THE

Ribbons

ARE FOR

Fearlessness

THE
Ribbons
ARE FOR
Fearlessness

My Journey from Norway to
Portugal beneath the Midnight Sun

CATRINA DAVIES

Skyhorse Publishing

For Naomi and Rosie, and all my other sisters

We have simply cheated ourselves the whole way down the line. We thought of life by analogy—as a journey or a pilgrimage—which had a serious purpose at the end. The thing was to get to that end, success, or whatever it is, or maybe Heaven after you are dead, but we missed the point along the whole way. It was a musical thing, and you were supposed to sing or dance while the music was being played.

—Alan Watts, *The Tao of Philosophy*

CONTENTS

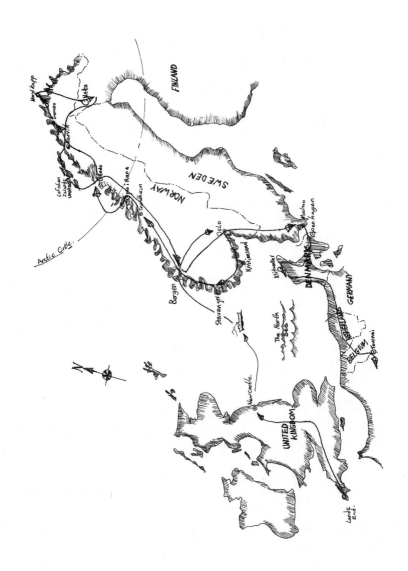

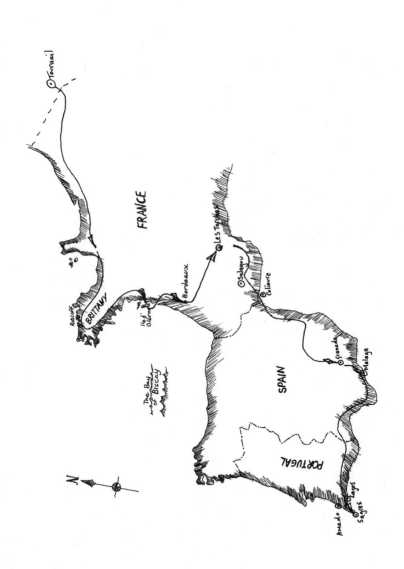

N

Tournai

FRANCE

BRITTANY

Roscoff

Iles d'Oleron

Bordeaux

Les Torches

Salgau

Collioure

The Bay of Biscay

SPAIN

PORTUGAL

Granada

Malaga

Amado

Sagres

Lagos

AUTHOR'S NOTE

Before we start our journey I'd like to say a few words about truth. It is true that in the summer of 2005 I drove an old yellow van on to a ferry bound for Norway, with a one-way ticket and a cello, intending to busk my way to Nordkapp and see the midnight sun. It is true that someone I had known for most of my life had died the previous year and that is what inspired me to undertake this crazy mission. It is true that I had a broken heart, that I had been in love and had lost. It is true that I survived for a year and traveled alone in my yellow van, through playing my cello on hundreds of streets, from Norway to Portugal. It is true that I met a girl who wrapped me up in light and gave me two ribbons, for fearlessness. I still have them. These are facts. When I first tried to write this book I didn't understand the relationship between facts and stories. I came up with something as long as *Ulysses* and not half as readable, where the truth was lost down endless cul-de-sacs of confusion and boredom, just as it is in life. So I tried again. I realized that the relationship between facts and truth in a story is not always clear-cut. Stories have their own internal logic, by means of which the truth emerges, and to find this truth the facts have to be sculpted and whittled down like a sculptor whittles a piece of stone, in order to expose the form hidden within. So I got very clear about the truth of my journey, the truth that I had experienced out there on the road, and then I allowed the needs of the story to take over. I fashioned single characters out of a cast of half a dozen. Important encounters were transplanted from one place to another. Names were changed. The conclusion was imported from the future. In my opinion this poetic use of the facts is not only justifiable but necessary, as it serves to make the truth shine more brightly.

INTRO

Since I got back and told the story of what happened, everyone keeps asking the same question; if I had known in advance how hard it was going to be, how many mountains I would have to climb, how many lonely roads I would have to drive, how many hours of music I would have to summon up from a part of myself I didn't even know existed, would I still have gone?

And perhaps I wouldn't.

It seemed daunting enough as it was. Busking my way to the midnight sun and back. With a cello. Which I had never played on the street. Or anywhere else, for that matter, apart from my bedroom. But I thought the whole thing would be over in a couple of months. I'd do it because I had to, for Andrew's sake, and then I'd carry on with my old life again. And nothing much would have changed, apart from Andrew, of course, and the fact that Jack would see I wasn't as pathetic as he thought I was and come back.

But that's not what happened. Everything changed. Because I met Hanna.

I tried to tell them about Hanna the day I returned, when we were finally all back at Broadsands, the backpackers' hostel near Land's End, in Cornwall, where I had lived and worked for several years before my great adventure. It was just like the old days. They took the piss.

"She sounds like a Bond girl."

"I'd give her one."

"Maybe if you gave her one you'd get ribbons, too."

I've thought about it often. How easy it would have been not to have met her. If I had been an hour later, or an hour earlier. If the fog hadn't lifted. If I hadn't called Ben from that phone box in Tromsø. If I hadn't met Henrik. If I hadn't ever left in the first place.

I don't believe in destiny, but nowadays I do believe in fearlessness.

I believe that there are well-trodden paths through life, paths made familiar by habit, or ancestors, or television, that bring us into contact with the things and the people we already know.

Paths that lead to the pub, the sofa, the supermarket, the job we're sick of but don't have the guts to leave, the houses we hate, the politics that don't serve us.

But I know now that there are other paths, too. Insane, impractical, ridiculous paths. Paths that are not familiar and do not feel safe, that have not been walked by celebrities, or friends, or anyone. And it's all too easy to ignore these paths, because to follow them requires a huge leap of faith, a fingers-in-your-ears, eyes-shut-to-the-consequences kind of fearlessness.

But if you do follow them, no matter how crazy they look to those on the outside, if you muster your courage and go, that's when you meet the people that change you. Like Hanna.

I never used to understand what fearlessness was. I thought that some lucky people, like Jack, were just born unafraid, and that was why they could surf huge waves and climb massive overhanging cliffs with no ropes. But real fearlessness has got nothing to do with being unafraid. It's about doing things anyway, getting on with it, living, whether you're afraid or not. And courage isn't about climbing huge cliffs with no ropes. Courage is about telling the story of who you are with your whole heart. Courage is about being who you are with your whole heart.

So I gave up trying to talk to them and instead I went to my van and got the ancient guitar that Francis Philippe had given me at Salagou, and I went back into the bar and I sat down and I started to play the chords from "Bruca Maniguá," the song that will always remind me of Hanna and that night we drove through the wilderness together. And then I started to sing the words I had finally finished writing on the long journey home. And it certainly shut them up. They stared at me like I was a freak of nature, and I could hardly blame them. I used to die of shame if one of them accidentally heard me playing my cello through the thick walls of the bunkhouse, and now here I was singing in public.

You said you wrapped me up in light that day,
You said you'd show me how to find my way,
You said these moments are all precious,
And the ribbons are for fearlessness . . .

It wasn't easy. I had to stop and take a big swig of Rattler, which is when I noticed they weren't taking the piss any more.

"What is that?" asked Ben. "It's really familiar."

"It's an old Cuban song. Ibrahim Ferrer did a cover. I used it loads busking. That girl I was trying to tell you about got me into it. In fact, this song is about her."

"How can an old Cuban song be about some girl you met in Norway?"

"They're my words."

Jack and Ben looked at each other.

"Start again from the beginning," said Jack.

Part One:

Love and Death

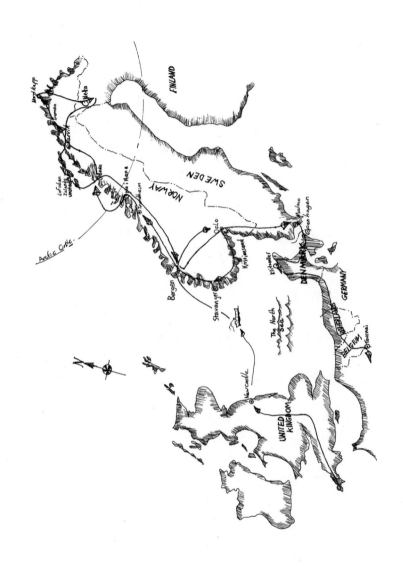

1

Beginnings are hard to pin down, because they're always overlapping with endings, but I suppose you could say that this particular story started where it finished, at Broadsands. Dawn was just breaking one midsummer morning. I said good-bye to Ben, who was running the place while the owner was traveling the world on a vast inheritance, and drove my bright yellow van 500 miles up the coast to Newcastle. At least, the bits that weren't brown from rust were bright yellow. Not the kind of yellow you'd find in a van factory, either. More the kind of yellow you might end up with if you were trying to disguise a stolen vehicle in a hurry and one of your mates had a spare can of spray paint.

Which is probably why the policeman pulled me over. He sucked air through his teeth and kicked one tire then another. I stuck the heels of my hands in my eyes and tried to focus on looking normal. If only I was someone else: the kind of person with the kind of happy-go-lucky approach to life that I would have cut off my own arm for. And sold my left leg. But I am not that kind of person. I am a worrier. And I had not taken my rattling, ancient van on this fourteen-hour journey from Land's

End to the Tyneside tunnel in order to spend twenty-four hours crossing the North Sea on a ferry bound for Norway because I was brave and fiercely independent, or because this was the type of thing I was in the habit of doing. I had done it for the same two reasons people have been doing everything for thousands of years: love and death.

I had only had the van for a couple of weeks. I had chosen it because it was all I could afford and because it was so old it had a tape player, so I would finally be able to listen to the six dusty tapes that were all the proof I had that Jack ever existed. It was a three-and-a-half-ton Iveco Daily with a medium wheel base, six tires, and loads of horsepower. Frankly, it felt like driving a forty-ton truck. Ben had got it cheap from his motorcross mates. It reeked of grease and old motorbikes.

Most people hadn't thought it would even manage this far, let alone what lay ahead. They raised their eyebrows and shook their heads and tried, not very successfully, to pretend they didn't think I was insane. It's true that it really didn't look like much. Apart from the rust and the spray paint it had a clutch that sounded like the noisy creaking of a coffin being opened by a vampire in the dead of night, a murderous sliding door that kept falling off and had already put nine stitches in my head, and two bald tires. Which I would have been more concerned about if they weren't on the back, where there were two each side. Ben called it a twin axle. I called it safety in numbers. Until the policeman pulled me over.

I attempted to muster a smile and waved my ferry ticket in his face to let him know I was leaving the country.

"Routine safety check."

My heart sank.

If only Jack were there. Golden-haired, broad-shouldered, rock-climbing, seductive, selfish Jack, who owned his selfishness with the pride of a religious convert. Jack didn't freak out every time he saw a police car. He didn't grip the steering wheel with sweating palms convinced he was about to be locked up for a crime he didn't even know he'd done. He gave policemen the finger and told them to their face they were pigs. But Jack was not there. Jack was about as far away as it was possible to be without actually being in space.

The policeman asked me to open up the back.

I was sitting in the driver's seat. The back doors didn't open from the outside, because they were broken. The side door was held on with cable ties. One thing to knock myself out, quite another to knock out a policeman doing a routine safety check. The only option was to squeeze myself through a small hole in the bulkhead, a sheet of metal that separated the cab from the back. Things went from bad to worse. For a few horrible seconds I thought the policeman was going to have to call the fire brigade. Then there was a loud bang as I landed headfirst on the floor.

The policeman peered inside. He looked at me and peered inside again. It was an unusual sight. The bare metal sides and rusty floor had been hastily cladded with splintered tongue and groove from the dump, until my new home resembled nothing so much as a disused sauna. Apart from the fact that there was no insulation and no heating. The fiberglass ceiling, which had not been cladded, was black with mold. Two pairs of jeans, four T-shirts, two warm sweaters, and some embarrassing pairs of underwear were stuffed into a piece of old fishing net Ben had found on the beach. An asymmetrical plywood offcut, with a washing-up-bowl-size hole cut into it and a secondhand gas cooker perched on top, was my kitchen. Apart from that there was a cupboard, which doubled as a bed. The policeman told me to open it. He scratched his head. Inside the cupboard, in an old beaten-up case, was my cello.

It may be eccentric but it is not actually illegal to drive around in a disused sauna with a cello under the bed. After warning me about my tires, the policeman let me go. I made it to the ferry just in time for a man in fluorescent overalls to measure the van with a ruler and wave me on board. Cars and trucks and shiny white campervans lined up behind me and switched off their engines. I sat motionless in the driver's seat, wishing I was a million miles away. Preferably on another planet, where life is like an old tape recorder and you can just record over the bits you don't like. Erase the mistakes, go back to the beginning, say the things you never said, do the things you never did. The massive metal doors, like a monstrous pair of jaws, clanged noisily shut behind me. My body felt heavy. Tears pricked my eyes. Because life is not like an old tape recorder. There is no pause button, no rewind button. No going back.

2

I had met Jack on the beach one winter's day.

I was tucked into the dunes watching the waves, which is something I did a lot. I liked watching them crash on the rocks and make patterns in the sand. I liked thinking about how far they must have traveled and where they might have come from. The Caribbean, or Alaska, or somewhere out in the middle of the ocean that had no name. It was raining slightly. I wore an old anorak. Jack didn't. Jack didn't care about things like rain. Jack came looming out of the mist with nothing but a backpack full of climbing ropes and a surfboard under each arm.

Broadsands had rooms with bunk beds, which Ben occasionally rented out to traveling surfers. It was in these rooms that Andrew and I lived. In exchange we would do a few hours of work behind the bar when it was busy, which it never was. Broadsands was a mile inland from the beach, just outside the tiny village where Andrew and I grew up. Most people who grew up in that village left as soon as they were old enough to buy a train ticket. Andrew and I had tried to leave, but we both came back. Andrew because he was addicted to surfing and me because I had no idea what I wanted to do, and because the sea is a hard thing to live without once it's in your blood.

Ben offered Jack a room, but Jack insisted on clearing out the shed at the bottom of the garden, which was six feet square and infested with mice and spiders. He covered the ancient rotting floor with beach mats, laid his Therm-a-Rest on top of them, and made a shelf out of driftwood for his novels by Aldous Huxley and Jack Kerouac, books of Japanese death poems and half a dozen old tapes nobody could listen to because who the hell has a tape player any more?

Every morning Jack brewed fresh coffee in a Bialetti espresso maker, which he balanced on an ancient Trangia, an alcohol-burning stove designed for high altitudes that made the whole place stink of petrol. He wore flowered shirts he bought in charity shops and his surfboards were stenciled with Japanese characters that meant things to him he couldn't explain. He called himself a wanderer and was full of stories of all these crazy adventures he'd been having since he was two years old, trailing round the world after his dad, who was something high up in the Marines.

My dad was not something high up in the Marines. My dad was funny, charming, lovable, saddened, and broken by a life that had been much harder than he'd expected. He built a business from nothing in the eighties and lost it all in the nineties. He drank subtly and relentlessly, and it didn't make him happy. With our house went my parents' marriage and, for a time, my mother's sanity. She had taught us all there was to know about love and we loved her fiercely in return. My sisters and I clung together and tried as hard as we could to pull her back from the cliff edge she teetered on, but there were days when she barely knew our names. Homeward journeys on the school bus were clouded with fear. The specter of suicide gnawed at us constantly. I grew up quickly and moved out early. My parents couldn't be burdened with my survival when they were fighting for their lives. Moreover, since we lost our house, my bedroom was a tent in the garden of my mother's tiny flat. I saw her often, but Broadsands became my home, and the people I knew there, like Ben and Andrew, became my family.

The school bus fear lingered into adulthood. Maybe that was why I fell so hard for Jack. Jack had no fear. He hurled himself at cliffs—like those sticky men you throw at windows when you're a child—and climbed them with no ropes. He paddled out to razor-sharp reefs nobody had ever dared to surf and grew hallucinogenic cacti that could kill you. While most men viewed Jack with a certain suspicion, all the girls I knew were in love with him. Which is why I was so utterly and completely stunned when he chose me. Plain old, fuzzy-haired, neurotic little me. I couldn't believe my luck. I was safe at last.

Only I wasn't.

Because one day, almost exactly a year later, Jack just got up and announced he was going to Patagonia.

"I need some time out."

He took everything. His books and shirts and Therm-a-Rest. His Patagonia duck down jacket. His climbing ropes. His Bialetti espresso maker and Trangia. Both his surfboards, and all the pieces of my shattered heart. The only remnants of our time together were the half dozen old tapes, which he said I might as well have, since he had no use for them, and one of his shirts that I hid because it smelled of him.

It killed me to think about it. It killed me to think about Jack's big, capable hands exploring some other girl's body.

But it killed me even more to think about Andrew.

Andrew with his stupid jokes and crazy dreams, his great big bags of leafy home-grown and his gift for making even the crappiest things seem funny.

Andrew was so far away it turned me inside out. But thinking about him was a really bad idea right then, even though this whole thing was his fault.

I sat paralyzed in the driver's seat.

Another man in fluorescent overalls tapped impatiently on the window. I gathered up a spare sweater and climbed several flights of echoing metal stairs until I found myself alone on the open deck. I leaned on the railings and watched as England shrank and vanished into the gray gloom. I stared down at the fizzing gray water and thought about my cello. I wondered how it felt about being stored like a sardine in a rusting yellow tin at the bottom of this huge ferry.

It had been mine since my grandfather had died when I was seven. Sometimes I felt like it was actually a part of me, like a leg or an arm. After Jack left I took it out of its case and put it on the floor by the blow-up mattress, so I would see it when I opened my eyes in the morning. Somehow this was comforting, which I suppose dated back to childhood. When things got tough for my family my cello was my best friend and my refuge. I told it everything. I was left alone to practice, and the melancholy music I gradually learned to play was like a lifeboat, pulling me through more storms than I cared to remember. Metaphorically speaking, of course. Until now.

It was raining. I went inside and found the room in which I had been allocated a reclining chair. I seemed to be the one and only passenger on the whole boat who had been unable to afford a cabin with a bed. Instead I had 150 reclining chairs and 150 purple nylon blankets, all to myself. I spread some of the blankets out on the floor and lay down under a huge sloping window. I watched angry gray clouds spit bursts of rain on the glass. I stood up. I sat down in one of the reclining chairs and stared at the wall and thought about my cello some more.

It was my cello that got me through the months after Jack left. I'd play in secret with my eyes half closed while tears dribbled out of them and made dull patches on the varnish. When I wasn't playing my cello in secret with my eyes half closed and tears dribbling out of them, I was sitting by the phone in Ben's shabby, chaotic office, staring into space, reading and rereading Jack's single text message—*I wish I could feel you naked beside me*—which only made the whole thing worse. Or lying in the shed on the cheap airbed I had bought that kept going flat, with my head buried in the shirt that already smelled more of damp than of him. Or scouring the second hand shops in Penzance for a tape player and trying not to think about him with beautiful, confident Argentinian girls sporting perfectly toned and tanned bodies. I used to love Broadsands. It used to feel like a refuge. After Jack left it felt like a prison.

Until the day that altered everything forever.

3

Jack had been gone three months.

I wandered into the bar. Ben was doing a crossword and smoking a joint.

Andrew was rolling another joint, a half-drunk pint of Guinness parked on the table next to him. I slumped on to a stool. Ben passed me the joint. I looked at it. All we ever did was drink and smoke. All over the world people like Jack were laughing and loving and surfing and climbing mountains and sleeping out under the stars and all we ever did was drink and smoke.

"Do you need a brandy?" said Ben.

"No." I shook my head. "I need to get out of this dump."

"Maybe it would help if you spent less time with your head in Jack's shirt."

He leaned over me to pour himself a pint of Doom Bar. "Don't you think it's time you got over it?"

"Yes,' I said, through gritted teeth. Sometimes I hated Ben. "Like I said. I need to get out of here."

"What's stopping you?"

"You don't pay us, that's what's fucking stopping me. I haven't got any money."

"Well, I haven't got any fucking customers."

Andrew passed me the other joint. I passed the one I already had back to Ben.

"I was watching telly the other night," said Andrew, breaking the tense silence. "It was a program about two guys who busked their way across America. They had an old van and a couple of guitars and they were pretty crap but they did it. All the way from Canada to Mexico."

Ben and I looked at each other. We knew what was coming.

"And I thought that's exactly what we should do. Sack this place off and be troubadours."

"What's a troubadour?" said Ben.

"A busker, you dickhead. A busker that travels. We could get an old van, like they did, and drive over to France and busk our way around."

I looked at him.

"Are you serious?"

"Of course he's not serious," said Ben. "He doesn't even play anything."

"I play the recorder," said Andrew, puffing out his chest. "Anyway, that's why we need Catrina."

He turned to Ben. "I thought you could be the one who goes 'round with a hat collecting all the money."

"Don't they normally get small children with missing limbs to do that?"

"You could dress up," said Andrew.

"Fuck off," said Ben, in his northern way. "I hate buskers. And France."

"You've never even been to France."

"I have."

That's when Andrew had his brainwave.

"We could go to Nordkapp!"

I stared at him. "Fuck!" I said.

"We could go to Nordkapp and see Jack's flipping midnight sun," said Andrew. "And it wouldn't matter that it was too expensive because we'd make all our money on the road."

Jack had a thing about Norway. According to him, it was just like New Zealand, only minus the backpackers, and close enough to drive to from England. He said one day he and I would get a van and fill it up with tins of food and drive it all the way to Nordkapp. I used to lie with my head on his shoulder and imagine myself safely strapped into the passenger seat while he took charge of everything. I'd picture the midnight sun, too, bouncing around in a sky full of stars, with reindeer wandering the cliffs and wondering what to do with themselves in all those hours of sunlight.

"Where the fuck is Nordkapp?" said Ben, who hadn't spent a lot of time listening to Jack.

"Most northerly point in Europe," Andrew and I said in unison.

"Uh, North Pole?"

"Is the North Pole in Europe?" Andrew looked at me. I shrugged my shoulders.

"Anyway, it doesn't matter," said Andrew. "The point is there's bears and reindeer and everything. It would feel like the North Pole."

"You're mental."

"Hey," said Andrew, practically jumping up and down with excitement, "we could go from Nordkapp to Cabo San Vicente."

"What's that?"

"It's a lighthouse in Portugal."

"A lighthouse in Portugal," said Ben, shaking his head. "Surely the other end would be Italy. The opposite of north is south, you know."

"Crap waves in Italy," said Andrew.

"I like Italy," I said, even though I'd never been there.

"I hate Norway," said Ben.

Andrew wasn't listening.

"We'd be free, out of the system, like the guy on that film who walked off on his own in Alaska and lived in an old lorry and ate berries."

"The one who died of starvation," said Ben.

"We're going to die anyway. It's getting shorter every day, you know."

"What is? Your dick?"

"This!" He waved his hand vaguely around the bar. "Life."

Ben snorted.

"That why you want to sit in a puddle of your own piss on street corners all over Europe playing 'Imagine' on a recorder, swigging wine out of a carton and kicking dogs."

"Busking is not the same as begging," said Andrew. "Busking is a public service. The government ought to pay people to do it. Stop them killing themselves after they've been shopping in Tesco."

"Catrina's cello makes me want to kill myself."

"He's right," I said, flushing with embarrassment. "You can't busk with a cello. It's much too big and sad."

"If you can hitch with a fridge you can busk with a cello." Tony Hawks was one of Andrew's heroes.

"Oh my God," said Ben. "Shut up about that stupid fridge. It's not funny any more. It never was funny."

"It's jazz. Hitching with a fridge is jazz."

"Why?"

"Shut up."

"You shut up."

There was a pause. I passed the joint back to Andrew.

"If you won't come with me," he said, through a mouthful of smoke, "I'll go on my own. I'm going to busk from Norway to Portugal before I die if it kills me."

I caught Ben's eye. We both tried not to laugh. The list of things Andrew was going to do before he died was longer than the Argos catalogue. Like us, he never actually did anything.

But then he did do something.

He died.

4

The reclining chairs were still all empty and the angry gray clouds were still spitting bursts of rain on to the sloping window. The door opened and a short, grayish, tough-looking man strode into the room, carrying a suitcase. He put the suitcase down on the floor and held out a hand for me to shake.

"Stan. Pub in London. Drive with the Arabs."

Stan needed a drink, and I knew that if I was left alone I would start crying and never stop, so I followed him to the saloon, which was full of noisy fruit machines and excitable teenagers. I slumped on a stool, my chin resting on my hands, while Stan necked tiny cups of instant coffee, chain-smoked cigarettes of a kind I had never seen before, and asked me a whole load of questions I didn't want to answer.

"What's a girl like you doing sleeping in a van all on her lonely, anyhow, heh heh?"

I shook my head and tried not to cry.

"Don't know. Good point." Stan roared with laughter, ordered another coffee and lit a cigarette. Among the smoke and the jukeboxes he had the commanding manner of an animal in its natural habitat.

"Got plenty of dosh have you? Not cheap over there."

"None."

"None?"

"I've got a cello." My voice shook slightly. "I'm going to busk my way to the midnight sun."

Stan bellowed with laughter. I thought about sticking a small plastic fork in his eye.

When he'd finished downing coffees Stan moved on to small plastic bottles of warm white wine. I was more enthusiastic about these. He watched approvingly as I knocked them back. He winked and held up a small fat hand for a high five.

"Where you headed then? South? East? You're not staying in Norway? Save the easy ones f'when you're old, heh heh."

I thought he *was* quite old.

"Reckon Helsinki first, then Moscow, Beijing, do China f'a couple weeks then Prague, see the Czechs, Athens, heh heh. Joke f'you. Lady asks a waiter how they prepare their chickens. Waiter says nothing special we just flat out tell 'em they're gonna die."

After they closed the bar we stumbled back to the room full of chairs. It was still empty.

I lay down on my pile of blankets and tried to read an ancient copy of *Europe on a Shoestring*, published in 1988, that Ben had kindly given me before I left. Stan was still chatting, presumably to himself.

"Get out as quickly as possible, buy a sandwich, heh heh, Stockholm, Helsinki, play with the Russians."

Europe on a Shoestring was full of dire warnings. In the section on Norway it told me that mobile homes were not allowed to overnight in rest areas ever. I told myself sternly that nobody in their right mind could possibly mistake my lurid yellow rust bucket for a mobile home. I trembled at the thought of it being towed away in the dead of night and crushed, with me sleeping peacefully inside. Or what if I was woken up by tall, blond Viking policemen wielding clubs? Although maybe that wouldn't be *as* bad. Jack always said I had chronic anxiety and an overactive imagination. I tried as hard as I could not to think about Jack, about the way he used to zip me up inside his Patagonia duck down jacket while he was wearing it, and how safe I'd feel, but the more I tried the worse it got. I pulled some purple nylon blankets over me and huddled under them. Stan started snoring and snorting and twitching in the corner.

What Jack liked about Norway was the fact that there weren't any people there.

"Norway has the lowest population density in the whole of Europe," he'd say, propping his beautiful head on a muscled arm and staring at me with his clean blue eyes.

"It's three times the size of England, but with less than a tenth of England's population. Do you know what that means?"

I didn't.

"Over here there are nearly four hundred people to every square kilometer. How many do you reckon there are over there?"

"I dunno. Two hundred?"

"*Eleven.*"

I picked up the book and turned to the driving section.

"Always carry a spare can of fuel because vast sections in the north are sparsely populated and gas stations are hundreds of kilometers apart."

I put the book down. I didn't even have a spare tire.

5

At midday on 17 June, almost twenty-four hours after it left Newcastle, the ferry docked in Bergen. Bergen is surrounded by a ring of seven mountains. It is also on the coast. If you have ever spent time in Wales you will know what that means. In an average year Bergen sees 294 days of rain. I arrived on one of those days. And it wasn't just any old rain. It was God on high with a pressure hose, desperately trying to purge the world of humans, who all had their heads down and on as they fought their way through the downpour.

The first thing I had to do was buy diesel. But before I could do that I had to change the fifty-pound note that had been a leaving present from Ben, who had done a whip 'round at Broadsands on one of the few occasions that the bar was busy. I parked the van and walked straight into the middle of a very busy fish market. Music blared from dozens of portable radios. Tall, blond men shouted and smiled and held out skewers with pieces of raw fish stuck on the end of them. In spite of the hostile conditions, everyone was stoically eating ice cream. I fought my way through the stalls and out the other side to a large square called Torgalmenningen, where I finally spotted a bank. It was closed. Across from it was another bank. This one was also closed. I summoned up the courage to ask a tall, blonde girl who looked like a supermodel if she knew why all the banks were closed. It was Saturday, she said, kindly, and with perfect English. I must go to the tourist office, on the Vagsallmeningen. She checked her watch. And I must hurry. The tourist office would also soon be closed.

I emerged half an hour later, sweating and soaking, with a handful of useless leaflets and four hundred and eighty two Norwegian kroner stuffed into the back pocket of my torn and faded jeans. That's when I realized I had absolutely no idea where I'd left the van.

Unfortunately I had left it in a bus stop. Uniformed officials were frowning and looking at the tires and writing things in notebooks, while a bus waited to pull in. There was a long line of traffic behind the bus. I tried to look as if I was about to cry, which was not very difficult. The officials glared at me and told me to fuck off in Norwegian. Or at least that's what I think they said.

The first garage was closed. The second had one of those low ceilings suspended in the air with lights hanging off it. I only remembered I was driving a forty-ton truck when a fat man came charging toward me shaking his fist. It was lucky he did. A few seconds later and I would have been driving a forty-ton truck with no roof. The third garage didn't take cash. By the time I reached the fourth garage, a bright orange Statoil, my hands were shaking like an alcoholic who had run out of wine. I handed over four hundred of the kroner, the equivalent of about forty pounds. The tank was just under half full. The rain hammered on the window.

"It is thirty degrees in Oslo," said the man, who was wearing orange overalls.

"How far is Oslo?" I croaked, as little rivers dribbled out of my sleeves and onto the floor.

"Oslo is five hundred kilometers," said the man.

Back in the van, while the rain hammered nervously on the fiberglass roof, I tried to work out if just under half a tank of diesel would be enough to get me 310 miles. I started the engine. There was only one way to find out.

Driving in Norway is very different to driving in England. Oslo and Bergen are the country's largest cities, but the road that connects them is smaller than the A30, with a speed limit that never exceeds 50 mph. What the road lacks in size, however, it more than makes up for in engineering. Desolate caves as long as the Channel Tunnel burrowed through the mountains, lit with creepy fluorescent green lights. Bridges straddled vast, salty rivers and there was so little traffic I began to wonder if I'd missed something important, like the fact that Norway was about to be hit by a massive earthquake and everyone should stay inside. At least navigation wasn't a problem. You could go north or south, with the occasional option of east or west. That was it. I went north for a while, then I went east. Then the rain finally stopped and I pulled into a lay-by, turned off the engine, filled a kettle with water from my jerry can, spilling most of it on the floor, lit my secondhand gas stove, opened the side door and sat staring at snowcapped mountains.

What the hell had I got myself into?

When I'd told people I was going to busk to Nordkapp and see the midnight sun, most of them had thought I was joking. Especially when I said it was Andrew's idea, and I was doing it for him. Something told me not to mention that it was also Jack's idea, and I was also doing it for him, to prove something, in the desperate hope that he would fall in love with me again and we would live happily ever after. Although it was hard to believe in happily ever after now that Andrew was dead.

Occasionally someone muttered excitedly about fjords, although nobody knew what a fjord actually was. Everyone had always wanted to see one anyway, but nobody ever had because it was too expensive. In short, I knew nothing about Norway and I knew nobody in it. Apart from a friend of a friend of a friend, that I had never met or spoken to, called Aase Gjerdrum. Aase lived in Oslo and worked for a Norwegian publishing company. I wondered what she would think if she knew that her phone number was taped to my dashboard, that I thought of her as some kind of guardian angel, and that I had nothing else to fall back on. I had no credit card, no AA membership, no Bank of Mum and Dad. Aase Gjerdrum was the sum total of my safety net.

The kettle boiled and I made a cup of tea from my stash of Yorkshire tea bags and carried it outside. I leaned against the side of the van, hating myself. If only I had actually tried busking before I left, like any normal person would. Instead I had listened to a very stoned Ben read out loud from Wikipedia. Apparently busking started in ancient Rome, although it was unclear exactly what the ancient Romans did, apart from wear flip-flops. "Busker," according to Ben, originally meant "flip-flop wearer." I looked down at my own flip-flops, what was left of them, which wasn't much. Later, the Spanish verb *buscar* came to mean "to seek or wander." Ben rolled his eyes, but I liked that. Jack would have liked that. The French version *busquer*, on the other hand, means "prostitute." In English, in my experience, busking usually meant sitting wearily on the pavement in the rain with a recorder, a dog, and a can of Special Brew.

I had convinced myself it would be easier in a foreign country with absolutely no chance of seeing anyone who even vaguely recognized me. Now, leaning against the van by that lonely fjord, miles from anywhere, I knew that it would not. It didn't matter if I was in England, Norway, or Timbuktu, I was the worst candidate for busking the world had ever seen. It's not that I couldn't play. Apart from at school, where the endless repetition of scales in front of teachers who were clearly bored out of their minds made me want to scratch my own eyes out with the bow, the trauma of music exams made me physically sick, and the humiliation of dragging the thing on to the school bus and having to sit with it in the front seat made me want to curl up and die, I had always loved my cello with the deep and lasting love you might have for a sibling. But my relationship with my cello was personal, and playing it was something I did alone, with my eyes closed, in darkened rooms, when I was absolutely certain nobody was listening. And what I played were elegies and requiems. Things that made me cry. Which would probably go down quite well at a funeral. But less well in a shopping center. I couldn't play anything else, either, because I didn't know anything else off by heart and I hadn't brought any sheet music with me. Ben had said it was naff to busk with a music stand. I emptied what was left of my tea on the ground and climbed back into the driver's seat. I put one of Jack's tapes in the tape player. Instead of playing, it chewed itself up and spat itself out.

6

The diesel warning light had been on for about 30 miles by the time I was relieved of half my life savings, about five pounds, by a man whose job it was to collect tolls from people wishing to enter Oslo, a practice I thought had died out in the Middle Ages. At least the man was kind. I enquired about places to park for the night and he told me about a lake called the Maridalsvannet, which doubled as an informal campsite for migrant workers. I arrived at dusk and they came in pairs with cans of beer to lean on my van and stare at me until I closed the door and lay down in my sleeping bag on my makeshift bed.

The man in the orange overalls had been right about the weather. I woke up in a much hotter country. I drove toward the center of the city and spent some time trying to find a place to park that wasn't ferociously expensive. In the end I left the van on a side street in front of a sign I didn't understand and hoped for the best. I had worse things to worry about. Unable to eat, sick with dread, I hauled my cello out of its cupboard and onto my back. They make cello cases out of carbon fiber now, light and shiny. Mine was made of plywood. The straps had long since broken and been replaced by leather belts that dug into my shoulders like an old-fashioned instrument of torture. I had a wooden stool with a hole in the top that could just about be carried in one hand. In the other hand I carried a red woollen beret. At the last minute I stuffed Aase Gjerdrum's telephone number into my back pocket.

Apart from a suprising number of girls in bikinis, Oslo was deserted. All the shops were closed and everyone was sunbathing—frantically, it seemed—stocking up on vitamin D after an unimaginably long and depressing winter. I wondered if there were public holidays for that kind of thing in Norway. There were sunbathers everywhere; on the pavements, on the grassy centers of major roundabouts, on flat roofs, on wooden benches, draped over stone statues. They propped themselves up and stared at me curiously as I shuffled past with my load, desperately wishing that, instead of the cello, I had learned to play something small and easy to hide, like the violin, or the kazoo.

I finally came to a halt by a big fountain at the entrance to the Nationaltheatret underground station. I found a shady corner and sat down on the stool. There were crowds of people milling around. I couldn't think of a single thing in the world I wanted to do less than unpack my cello in front of them, let alone play it. But if I didn't want to spend the rest of my days in Oslo, slowly starving to death, that is what I had to do. I tightened the bow and let the spike out. Some of the people had stopped milling around and were looking at me. I wondered if busking was illegal in Norway. I took out the cello, dropped the hat on the ground and tried to smile. Nobody smiled back. There was a noise in my ears like the sea.

I decided to play the Minuet from the first Bach Suite, because it was easy, because it was famous, and because it was the only thing I could remember in a major key. Major keys are the ones that sound cheerful, as opposed to minor keys, which sound mournful. Needless to say, almost everything I knew by heart was in a minor key.

It didn't go well. There are no frets on a cello, and finding the right place for my fingers on the strings when my hands were sweating and shaking from adrenaline was virtually impossible, even if I had remembered to tune up first, which I hadn't. Somehow I made it to the end, then I dropped the bow, reached down to pick it up and was nearly sick on the floor. I spotted a phone box on the other side of the fountain. I thought about calling Ben and asking to borrow the money for a ferry ticket home.

Two children came and stood in front of me, giggling and pinching each other. Their mother came and smacked them and put two coins in the hat. I tried to say thank you, but when I opened my mouth no words came out. I began to wonder if I was clinically insane. I got up off the stool, put my cello back in its case, stuffed the two coins, which amounted to twelve kroner, about one pound twenty, into my back pocket, picked up the stool and the hat and walked toward the phone box. Twelve kroner wasn't enough to call Ben and ask to borrow the money for a ferry ticket home. I focused on trying to unlock my jaw, which was clamped shut so hard my teeth were beginning to hurt.

I walked and walked, oblivious to my surroundings. I walked until I found myself on the edge of what I later found out was the Oslofjord. I sat down under a huge poster of *The Scream* by Munch. I tried to gather my thoughts, while yachts tugged at their moorings and huge cruise ships drifted at anchor like floating blocks of flats, and people ate ice cream and other people drank cold beers at cafés with colorful umbrellas. I realized that I was hungry. A dark-skinned boy with several missing teeth handed me a piece of paper with his telephone number on it. I wondered if twelve kroner was enough for an alcoholic drink.

Twelve kroner was not enough for an alcoholic drink, but it was enough for a phone call to Aase Gjerdrum. I almost cried when she said that I had chosen the right time to call. It was Sunday (which explained all the closed shops and sunbathers), she was not at work, and she had time to come and meet me at the Oslofjord. We went to one of the cafés with colorful umbrellas. Aase ordered two bottles of Arctic beer and some salmon sandwiches, then she spread a big map of Norway out on the table.

"So that we can pore over it," she said, her handsome face lighting up.

I knew that Aase was married to a famous Norwegian author. I didn't know that her son, Erling Kagge, was a famous Norwegian explorer. The first man in history to make it to the North Pole, the South Pole, and the summit of Everest.

"He has sailed across the Atlantic, around Cape Horn, to the Antarctic and the Galapagos Islands." Aase smiled brightly. "When he went to the South Pole he did not even take a radio."

I hid behind my salmon sandwich.

"He has just written a book. It is called *Philosophy for Polar Explorers*."

I picked up my Arctic beer.

"Where are you staying?"

I mentioned the Maridalsvannet. Something told me not to mention the migrant workers.

"You are camping?"

I had emailed Aase before I left. She knew about my plan to busk to the midnight sun. Maybe she had thought I would be staying in hotels.

"I have a van. A bright yellow van."

"You are driving?" She shook her head. "I hope you have plenty of time. The roads are not so good in the north and the distances are very vast."

I took a large gulp of Arctic beer.

"Do you know much about Norway?"

"I know there are hardly any people."

"Yes, that is true, and more than half live here in the southeast. Stavanger and Bergen are also important cities. In the north, after Trondheim, there is practically no one."

On reflection, it didn't seem like the ideal place to launch a busking career.

Aase spread the map out on the table and pointed to things as if I were a wealthy tourist instead of a homeless beggar who had undertaken an impossible task.

"The fjords are a must, of course, and the national parks are wonderful. I have never been to the Polarsirkelen myself. It is too far."

I said nothing.

"Would you like some more food?"

Aase ordered three slices of cake and two more bottles of Arctic beer. It was a relatively new thing, she said, being able to buy beer in a café. The prohibition lasted well into the 1950s.

"We were still a very drunk country, though," she said, encouragingly. "People simply made illegal distilleries in their houses."

According to Aase, Arctic beer was brewed in the northernmost brewery in the world in the northernmost university town in the world. Tromsø.

"We call it the Paris of the north."

"Why?"

"You will see!"

I swallowed.

"How far is Tromsø from here?" I said.

"About two thousand kilometres."

I took a huge gulp of beer.

"You know what. I don't actually think I'm . . ."

My voice trailed off.

"Do you know what the other name for Erling's book is?"

"No," I said.

"All the things they do not teach you in school!"

She patted my hand.

"You see, Erling was not top of the class. Or even the best at gym. He was just a dreamer. And that is what they do not teach you in school."

"To be a dreamer?"

"To believe in your dreams."

Aase left. I wrapped the spare piece of cake in a napkin and stuffed it into my cello case. I drank the last of the Arctic beer and carried my cello onto one of the wooden boardwalks that ran alongside the fjord. I put the stool down and sat where I could see the water. I put out the red woollen beret, even though the boardwalk was entirely deserted, and too far from the cafés for anybody there to be able to hear me. That's why I had chosen it. I needed some time alone with my cello. I tuned up and launched into the Minuet again, eyes closed, rehearsing it for the next time I went out onto the street. By the third rendition it sounded almost like music. Halfway through the fourth I heard a cough. I opened my eyes.

"You need money?" said a pig-like man with gold rings on his fat fingers.

He stank of aftershave and had a thick accent that could have been Russian. I nodded. I pushed the beret toward him with my toe. The man laughed, showing a small, pink tongue and several gold teeth. He felt in his pockets and pulled out a great big handful of coins, which he threw in the beret. I stared at him.

"I am rich man," he said.

I tried to smile. He leaned in close. Too close.

"I have boat. You spend twenty-four hours with me on boat I give you ten thousand kroner."

I gasped. Ten thousand kroner was a thousand pounds. A thousand pounds was enough to get me all the way to Nordkapp. And back, probably. And drink Arctic beer at cafés with colorful umbrellas, and eat smoked salmon sandwiches and cake. No busking, in other words. Ever again. The man was drumming his fingers together.

"But what would you want me to do," I asked, stupidly.

He stuck his face right next to mine.

"Eversing," he whispered.

7

The great big handful of coins amounted to three hundred kroner, about thirty pounds. Not enough to get to Nordkapp and back but enough, thankfully, to get out of Oslo. I was in such a hurry to do this that I ended up on the wrong road and found myself traveling not north, as I had originally planned, or even west, back to Bergen, but south, toward a town called Kristiansand. As far away as you can get from Nordkapp, in other words, without actually leaving the country. By the time I realized what I had done it was too late to turn around.

I spent my second night by the sea, parked above a sandy cove. I arrived late but it was not dark. Instead the sky was an inky blue and the air was heavy with the scent of roses and pine needles. The water looked so clear and clean it inspired in me a profound longing to wash. My skin felt sticky and uncomfortable, as though the events of the past days and weeks had attached themselves to it like burrs. My feet were black with dirt from tramping around Oslo in flip-flops. My hair was lank and greasy.

The water was freezing, much colder than Cornwall, but in spite of this I stayed in for ages, scrubbing my skin over and over with handfuls of sand. Afterward I ate pasta and tinned tomatoes that I had brought with me from England, sitting on the bed and watching the sky finally turn from an inky blue to a kind of dusky blue. I liked the cove, and I allowed myself to consider the possibility of not going to Nordkapp. Instead I would stay in the south, live on pasta, and slowly busk my way back to Bergen, where I would save the money for a ferry home. If I even managed that it would be a miracle, but at least if I wasn't racing to the midnight sun I could take as long as I liked. I tried not to think about Andrew, or Jack, or telling Ben that I'd only made it as far as Oslo.

One night turned into seven. The cove was called Galgebergtangen, which means Gallow's Point in English. Each morning a squad of old ladies wearing rubber swimming hats plunged like seal pups into the icy water. I ate pasta for breakfast, lunch, and dinner. I watched the longest day of the year come and go, only this time it was the longest day of my whole life, with barely two hours of darkness, and even then it wasn't really dark, just sort of dusky. I read all the books I had brought with me and practiced the first sixteen bars of the first movement of Haydn's *Cello Concerto in C*, which I could just about remember and which, like Bach's Minuet, was in a major key. I couldn't remember the rest of that movement. The second movement I knew all the way through, because it was a heartbroken, minor key adagio. Much too melancholy for busking.

On the third day I forced myself to drive to Kristiansand, about a mile away, and set up on the Strandpromenaden. I'd like to tell you that it went better this time, but I would be lying. My hands were still slippery with adrenaline and I kept losing my place in the music, because every time I opened my eyes there were people staring at me. At least they couldn't hear it. Nobody could hear it. I couldn't even hear it. Kristiansand is a noisy town and the cello is a quiet instrument. I made about a hundred kroner a day, the equivalent of ten pounds, from people who obviously felt sorry for me.

When I wasn't busking I was worrying. I worried incessantly. Mainly I worried about money. It's not that I wasn't used to having no money. I'd grown up with no money and I'd had no money ever since. It was one of those things about Cornwall. Nobody ever had any money. But it's one thing to have no money in the place you grew up where there are friends around the corner to lend you some if you are actually starving, and quite another to be alone with no money in a strange Norwegian town with nothing apart from one Minuet and the first sixteen bars of the Haydn *Cello Concerto in C*. When I wasn't worrying about starving to death, I was worrying about breaking down or breaking my cello. I worried about breaking myself, fatal van accidents, and having no busking licence. I worried about not knowing enough Norwegian to even find out if I needed a busking licence. I worried about Jack falling off some cliff somewhere on the other side of the world and I worried about Ben going stir crazy all alone at Broadsands. I worried that I would give myself a heart attack from worrying. And then, just before that happened, I met Jan Erik.

8

It was another hot and distinctly un-northern day. A couple of policemen, summoned by a shopkeeper who was threatening to shoot me and then himself if he ever had to hear the first sixteen bars of the Haydn *Cello Concerto in C* ever again, suggested that it might be time for me to leave Kristiansand. They were sympathetic, and they didn't mention anything about needing a licence. Instead they suggested I went to Stavanger, a couple of hundred kilometers up the west coast. It was Norway's third city, they said. The center of the oil industry. I'd do well there. Everyone was rich.

I had managed to save four hundred kroner, about forty pounds, which should have been more than enough to pay for the diesel I needed to travel a mere 125 miles. I chose what looked like the shortest route. I hadn't bargained for the topography. I was not yet familiar with the fact that roads in Norway are not so much roads as a series of bridges interspersed with boats. Three times the road ground to a halt in front of a large body of water and everyone stood leaning against their cars in the sun while a teenager came along and sold tickets for a clanging white ferry that was chugging slowly across the fjord. It was like going back in time. And there was no way out of it.

By the time I had driven on and off two ferries I was all out of spare cash. In the queue for the third I was reduced to hunting around on the floor of the van for bits of money I might have dropped. When I started hunting on the tarmac outside the van a long, thin man unfolded himself from the car in front. He said "heck" a lot, introduced himself as Jan Erik, and offered to pay for my ticket. Like everybody else, he wondered why I was traveling alone.

"I like traveling alone," I said, bravely.

"You are on holiday?"

"Well," I said. "A working holiday."

"Heck, why is that?"

"Because I have no money."

Jan Erik was enthusiastically discouraging.

"I hope you have got a visa! Norway is not part of the EU. Gray work is not easy to find. Heck, what do you plan to do?"

"I have a cello. I'm going to busk my way to Nordkapp and see the midnight sun . . ."

My voice trailed off. Something inside me gave a hollow laugh. Jan Erik crinkled his eyes again.

"What does it mean, busk?"

"Play music on the street."

Jan Erik shook his head.

"Like a troubadour."

"Troubadour?"

I tried to sound nonchalant.

"You know, one of those guys with a hat and a dog and a guitar with five strings. Only I've got a cello instead. Don't they have people like that in your town?"

"Stavanger? Heck, no. I have never seen a troubadour in Stavanger."

He crinkled his eyes again.

"You are going to drive all the way to Nordkapp and sleep in your car and play a violoncello in the street?"

I gritted my teeth.

"Actually it's a van."

Jan Erik looked at me with barefaced fascination.

"Did you know that it is as far to drive from Oslo to Tromsø as it is to drive from Oslo to Rome?"

"I'm not going to Tromsø. I'm going to Nordkapp."

"Nordkapp is even further! Do you know how far it is to Nordkapp?"

"About two thousand five hundred kilometers."

He nodded enthusiastically. I wanted to punch him.

"How much kilometers does your car make in the liter?"

I had spent lots of time on this.

"It'll go about one hundred kilometers on ten pounds which is . . ."

". . . one hundred kroner so that's about one kroner per kilometer plus ferries and tolls and mountains, which will be more expensive, so that's going to be, that's going to be, at least . . ."

Jan Erik did some maths in his head. He looked like the kind of person who enjoyed doing maths in his head.

". . . at least six thousand kroner!"

"Plus food," I said, weakly.

Jan Erik looked horrified. He took a pen out of his breast pocket and a piece of paper from his briefcase and proceeded to write down his phone number next to a map of where he lived in Stavanger.

"Give me a call," he said. "Heck, I will feed you."

He fed me steak. With it we drank a whole bottle of expensive red wine. I did not normally drink whole bottles of expensive wine in the houses of strange men, but somehow Jan Erik was different. He crinkled his eyes. If he hadn't been quite so long and thin I might have snogged him when he handed me an armful of soft clean towels and pushed me into a plush bathroom with a shower whose head was bigger than mine. And I would definitely have snogged him when he insisted on pasting a big piece of paper to the windscreen of my van saying, in Norwegian, that it was his and not to tow it away. (All the other vehicles in the car park were made by Mercedes or BMW and under two years old.) Jan Erik said I could sleep outside for as long as I wanted and use his shower. Heck, he said, I could sleep inside if I liked, in a bed, but I'd probably rather be in my car, seeing as I was a troubadour.

Jan Erik worked for a company that designed industrial computers for oil rigs. Only what he actually did every day was marketing.

"Heck, all jobs today are basically marketing."

"Except busking," I said, my mouth full of steak and my head full of wine.

He raised his glass.

"Except busking."

In the daytime Jan Erik wore a suit and worked in an office, selling things to do with oil. The rest of the time he was outside. His apartment was littered with skis. Like Jack, he had climbing ropes hanging from all his coat hooks. Unlike Jack, he never mentioned them. It was Jan Erik who told me that fjords were huge river valleys carved out by glaciers at the end of the last Ice Age. They snaked inland for hundreds of kilometers, often deeper than the sea. Hence the ferries.

The first evening he fixed my doors. Both of them, so that the back door opened from the outside and the sliding one slid and was not held on with cable ties. Jan Erik liked my van. He liked my red tin teapot and the ancient biscuit tin decorated with brown and orange flowers that I had taken to stashing kroner in.

"Heck," he said.

The second evening he produced a pair of sea kayaks, showed me how to paddle without falling out (not as easy as it looks) and led me up the Stavangerfjord to an uninhabited island where we cooked sausages over a fire he made by rubbing two sticks together. No kidding.

On the third evening we went to Gamle Stavanger, the old town, which was like walking round a museum-full of flowers in wooden tubs and higgeldy-piggeldy wooden cottages and ancient communal water pumps. Then we went to watch the final of the Grand Slam beach volleyball event.

"I bet you didn't expect to find the Grand Slam beach volleyball in Norway."

He was right. If I had thought about it, the Grand Slam beach volleyball was probably the very last thing I had ever expected to find in Norway.

"They make the sand expressfully," he said.

I think he meant especially.

"Real sand isn't good enough."

I expect you're thinking that I spent my days busking. I expect that's what Jan Erik thought, too. He gave me a key in the expectation that I would go out and come back. What I actually did was lie in the sun reading his books about other people climbing Everest. I told myself it didn't matter, now that I had given up on going to Nordkapp.

Until the fourth evening, when Jan Erik asked if I'd like to use his telephone to call home. He disappeared into the kitchen and left me alone in the hall. I dialed the number for Broadsands. It rang for ages. My heart smashed against my rib cage. Finally Ben answered.

"Hello," I croaked.

"How's troubadouring then?"

"Um, I . . ."

"Everyone thinks you're really brave."

I was taken aback. That was not the kind of thing I was used to hearing from Ben.

"Do they?"

"Jack called."

My knees went weak. I sat down on the floor.

"Is he okay?"

"He's working on some organic farm. Hates it."

Ben paused.

"Told him about Andrew. Says he's coming back."

I nearly dropped the phone.

"Told him you were busking to Nordkapp."

Ben couldn't keep the note of satisfaction out of his voice.

"What did he say?"

"Says it's as far to drive from Land's End to Nordkapp as it is to drive from Land's End to Baghdad. Says you'll never make it."

I could see Jan Erik pretending not to listen in the kitchen. I tried to breathe normally.

"Did he say anything else?"

"Said if you do make it he'll be bloody impressed."

9

Jan Erik owned a sleek yacht he'd bought in Plymouth and sailed across the North Sea single-handed. When Saturday came around again and I was still there, Jan Erik invited me to take part in a race he had entered. The marina was bustling with people. The yacht was so sleek and streamlined there was nowhere to actually sit, apart from the thin metal string that passed as railings and was so close to the water I was sure that if I leaned or sat on it I would fall in and be mashed up by the propeller.

Crinkling his eyes so much they practically disappeared, Jan Erik introduced me to the other crew. There were six of them, all men, wearing lightweight suits and dark glasses and lounging on the deck, smoking cigars. Jan Erik disappeared into the cabin to fiddle with complicated electronic instruments. One of the men offered me a cigar and told me to sit down. I balanced myself precariously on the thin metal string.

"Have you been sailing before?"

"Never."

They all laughed, suavely.

"Then I am sure today will be very interesting."

We were late to the starting line. The men rushed around unfolding sails and tying knots while I tripped over ropes trying to keep out of the way. When we were ready to go Jan Erik handed me a life jacket and taught me the Norwegian for now *(na)* and move *(flytte)*. *Flytte na!* When I heard either of those words I had to duck so as to avoid being accidentally beheaded by the heavy metal boom as it swung at speed across the deck whenever we changed direction.

At the crack of the starting pistol Jan Erik turned into a military dictator. He shouted and ran around and the other men shouted back and started fighting with ropes and then one of them got hit by the boom and staggered into the cabin to lie down, holding his head in both hands. Everyone ignored him and carried on shouting and running around and crashing into each other in the tiny space. Everyone took everything very seriously and everyone apart from Jan Erik was smoking a cigar the whole time.

There were sixty-five boats in the race, all different shapes and sizes. Jan Erik explained that they were judged differently, according to their different speeds. We traveled miles out into the open sea, all sixty-five boats sporting half a dozen people hanging on for dear life, sitting on rails that leaned at an alarming angle. Suddenly a huge orange tanker appeared out of nowhere and plowed straight toward us, dwarfing the yachts, which peeled off in all directions to avoid being mown down. It was chaos, like a scene from a disaster film about the insignificance of man in relation to oil.

After the race was over, we pulled in the sails and drifted. Although we had lost miserably, Jan Erik cracked open a bottle of champagne. Perspiring foreheads were wiped with clean white handkerchiefs. I asked the men what they did for a living and they told me they all worked in oil, apart from one, who was an investment banker. We raised our glasses to oil.

"*Scholl.*"

"What will you do when it runs out?"

"They keep finding more," said the investment banker. "Plus we are making a lot of money from the sovereign investment fund. We have the largest capital reserve of any nation in the world."

"Where is it?"

I glanced at the water, as if expecting it to be liquid gold.

"It's in shares and things all over the world."

"What if some economy crashes somewhere and you lose it all?"

They roared with laughter.

"Norway loses all her money on the stock exchange!"

"What would happen?"

The investment banker looked delighted.

"American invasion!"

They roared with laughter again and held up their glasses of champagne.

"*Scholl.*"

"To the stock exchange."

"What about you?"

The man who had been hit by the boom had nice eyes. There was a pregnant silence. Unfortunately, Jan Erik spoke up on my behalf.

"She is going to sleep in her car and play her cello on the street all the way to North Cape."

There was a long silence.

"Why?" someone said, at last.

I stared at them. Since that long night on the ferry I had managed not to think about it. I had been too busy running away, too busy worrying about busking, wondering how I was going to survive, and how on earth I was ever going to get to Nordkapp. But suddenly, out there on that boat, full of champagne, I knew that no amount of running away was ever going to make any difference. Jack would always be gone, and Andrew would always be dead.

Jan Erik's sleek yacht was still drifting on the fjord.

"How did it happen?" said the man with nice eyes, finally.

I blew my nose on my sleeve.

"That's the worst part. Andrew was an idiot. He'd get drunk and surf the roof of his car while someone drove it through the village, or borrow a rowing boat and take it out in a huge swell and tip it over in the shorebreak. He fell over the railings by the beach once, fell twelve feet on to rocks and just stood up and walked away. Then he went and died doing something we all did every single day. He died walking to the beach. The road's less than a mile long. There are speed bumps. And he got himself knocked over and killed by a car going at 20 mph. They said at the inquest that it wasn't the driver's fault. It was dark. It's hard to know what really happened."

Nobody spoke.

"Anyway, I'm not going to busk all the way to Portugal," I said. "That's ridiculous."

Still nobody spoke.

"But I did want to see the midnight sun."

I thought of it again, bouncing around in a sky full of stars. I thought of Jack, propping himself up on one arm in bed and looking at me with his clean blue eyes, and I thought of Andrew and how excited he'd been that day in the bar. The day he died. And the sadness was like a physical thing, like someone had punched me really hard in the stomach. And I knew I couldn't go home.

I couldn't let Andrew down, and I couldn't give Jack the satisfaction of saying I told you so.

"I do want to see the midnight sun."

The man with nice eyes handed me his handkerchief.

"I feel like I kind of owe it to Andrew. Which is stupid, isn't it? He's dead."

Dead.

I blew my nose. I was vaguely aware of Jan Erik standing in the doorway to the cabin.

"But it's too late now."

"I do not think it is too late," said the man with nice eyes. "It is only the twenty-sixth of June. You have until the twenty-ninth of July at Nordkapp."

I shook my head.

"Honestly. You don't understand. It takes me ten hours to make a hundred kroner. It's impossible."

"You can see it in other places too, that are not so far, but you have less time."

I stopped staring at the fjord and looked at him.

"Can you?"

"In Bodø [he pronounced it *Buddha*] you have until the twelfth of July."

"How far is Bodø?"

"One thousand five hundred kilometers."

I sighed.

"Or there is Tromsø. There you have until the twenty-second of July."

I remembered Aase saying that Tromsø was the Paris of the north.

"But Tromsø is two thousand kilometers."

"Two thousand one hundred and ninety five."

"How come you know all this?"

"I always wanted to drive up into the Polarsirkelen and see the midnight sun, too."

"And did you?"

"No."

10

Back at Jan Erik's house I finally started to get my act together.

Jan Erik had an album of smooth jazz classics (he was that kind of guy) and I began by learning "Summertime" and "Autumn Leaves." They were vaguely familiar to me and I was hoping that they would also be familiar to people on the street and that because of this they would give me money. It sort of worked. I'd never played jazz before and I liked the fact that I could just make it up if I got lost and people would assume I was improvising. I'd always thought I'd be crap at improvising, but it was easy. Much easier than having to get every note of Bach's Minuet exactly right, with the critical voices of childhood teachers running through my head. Every morning, no matter how much I didn't want to, I caught a bus into the center of Stavanger and set up next to the temporary volleyball courts, where crowds of tourists stood watching muscular men bounce balls over nets.

Busking didn't exactly get easier, but the more I did it the less adrenaline I had and the more I was able to relax. And when I was relaxed I played better. Sometimes people would even stop and come close enough to actually listen, at which point I would usually fluff all the notes. But I was learning. I learned to place a few coins in the hat to get things going, and to take coins out when it looked as though things were going too well. I learned to smile real smiles, so that people actually smiled back, and I learned to say thank you without losing my place in the music. A week later I decided I had enough coins in the biscuit tin to make the journey back to Bergen.

Leaving the safety of Jan Erik's car park felt like boarding the ferry from Newcastle all over again. He made me a packed lunch of bread and cheese and sausages and gave me a tape he had recorded of the smooth jazz classics, so I could play it in the van. I took a final hot shower.

"Heck," he said, and looked as if he was about to cry.

"Maybe I'll come back," I stammered. "After I've seen it."

Jan Erik shook his head.

"I think you are like a bird," he said. "A bird you cannot catch."

I tried not to imagine Jack bent double with laughter.

It was still raining in Bergen. As I sloshed around the wet streets looking for a pitch that wasn't waterlogged, the looming gray sky felt like the lid of a coffin and I couldn't stop thinking about Andrew.

Dead.

How could Andrew be dead?

I remembered that awful moment when Ben had opened the door and told me. He was actually crying.

Dead?

The days and weeks immediately after it happened were the strangest of my life. Ben said we were in shock. For me it was more like vertigo. Like being stuck halfway up a cliff. Like the time Jack tried to take me climbing and I couldn't look down or up but had to stare straight ahead at the rock, flattened against it like a cartoon animal that had just been shot out of a catapult, until he came and rescued me. Only this time there was nobody to rescue me. Jack wasn't there. And even Jack couldn't rescue me from death.

Everything looked different. It was as if I was looking at life through a different lens, and the odd thing was, it shone more brightly. The sky seemed bigger than it had been, and more blue. The birds sang more loudly. Sleep was out of the question. Instead I lay in bed for hours, my head throbbing with incomprehensible words like *nowhere*, *never*, and *nothing*. I spent hours on the beach staring at the waves. Andrew is nowhere. Andrew is never coming back. Andrew is nothing. And no matter what I did or didn't do, one day I would also be nothing. Which is possibly why I woke up one day and bought a one-way ticket to Norway. And why I spent the sum total of my very meager savings on a rattling old van that used to belong to Ben's motorcross mates.

It was raining so much I decided to try busking in a public toilet. It smelled of piss, but at least it was dry. I took my cello out of its case and played "Summertime" very badly. I stopped and opened my eyes. Three women were staring at me. Only when they left did I realize I had forgotten to put out the hat.

The next day I found some old wooden tunnels that ran between expensive craft shops in Bryggen, Bergen's answer to Gamle Stavanger. They were near the fish market. Right opposite the bus stop where I left my van that first day and came back to find it surrounded by uniformed officials. The tunnels in Bryggen were very old, and very crooked, and very empty. But they had roofs, and every half hour or so a Japanese tourist would poke his head in, bow apologetically as if he had interrupted me, and throw ten or twenty kroner in the hat. Which could have been worse, frankly. Until a fat woman in an apron came along and started shouting at me.

"Stop! Stop! Are you Russian?" she asked.

"No."

"Well. Stop anyway. Nobody is buying anything."

She drew her hand across her neck. "If you do not stop I will call the police."

Which wasn't exactly encouraging.

On the third day I got lucky. I found a subway. It was a long subway that led to the train station. It was dry and full of people. The only downside was that Tommy was already in there, strumming a guitar and singing a Bob Dylan song. Tommy looked about fifty but was actually thirty-four. What remained of his wispy hair grew on the very edges of a shiny red scalp. He wore black leather and cowboy boots, came from Newcastle, and had a dog on a piece of string. Tommy had seen it all. Except for a young girl on her own, busking with a cello. He let out a huge guffaw.

"That's a bloody big guitar."

I nodded and squelched closer. My ancient hiking boots, which were all I had apart from flip-flops, were so wet it was like having a small paddling pool attached to each foot. Tommy said I could have the spot while he went for lunch.

In sharp contrast to the noisy streets I had become accustomed to, where I had to saw away with the bow just to be able to hear myself, the tunnel was like a giant microphone crossed with an echo chamber. In that tunnel, everyone was going to hear it. I took a deep breath and launched into "Autumn Leaves." To my great surprise it actually sounded good. And because it sounded good I closed my eyes and really listened, and then it sounded even better. Through my half-closed eyes I could see people grinning as they walked past. More excitingly, I could hear the steady clang of coins dropping into the hat.

Tommy came back with two polystyrene cups of instant coffee. He handed me one of the cups.

"Thanks. That's kind of you."

"Got to stick together. What with this bloody cashless society."

A nice-looking man in a brown duffel coat came over, winked, and handed me a fifty-kroner note.

A fifty-kroner note!

"What?" I said to Tommy, staring at the note.

Tommy's eyes glinted.

"They hate music. Hate it. Scared, you see. Of crying."

I pushed the fifty-kroner note right down to the bottom of the back pocket of my jeans, so I would be in absolutely no danger of losing it. I noticed that Aase Gjerdrum's telephone number was still in there. I took a slurp of coffee, which was so sweet I spat it out again. Tommy had already finished his.

He screwed up the cup and chucked it on the ground. I began to scoop up the coins in the hat and stuff them into my other back pocket.

"Do all right?"

"Looks like it."

I couldn't stop grinning. In the hat was what looked like more money than I had ever seen in my entire life. Probably because it was all in denominations of about one pence. But still. Tommy looked me up and down.

"You can't half play."

I flushed.

"What are doing on the street?"

I lifted my chin.

"I'm going to Nordkapp to see the midnight sun."

Tommy let out another huge and heart-wrenching guffaw.

"Did that once."

"Really?"

"Got as far as Tromsø."

"The Paris of the north," I said, still high on the fifty-kroner note.

"More like Lima. So many panpipes half of 'em could go and have lunch and the other half wouldn't even notice. Never stopped. Only place I've ever played and made nothing. Nada."

"How did you eat?"

"Sold helium balloons."

I swallowed.

"I'd better go."

"Come back later if you like. After five."

He beckoned me close.

"It was like this," he whispered, spitting slightly in my ear. "Chap called George Burns got it right. Sometimes they throw something in the hats. Sometimes they take something out of the hats. Sometimes they take the hats."

11

After a week in Bergen, playing in the subway whenever Tommy had a break, there were enough kroner in the biscuit tin to start heading north. This was no mean feat. According to Aase's map the next town of any size was Trondheim, 435 miles away. Taking into account all the ferries, I calculated that it would take me at least three days to get to Trondheim. Three days of not having to busk.

I was in high spirits. When the ring of seven mountains was behind me, the rain stopped and the summer sun lit up the achingly beautiful scenery. I could see everything, being much higher up in the van than I would have been in a car, and what I saw was a magical land of drifting fjords, clapboard houses and gnarled apple trees, hay barns on stilts, ancient tractors, and trestle tables groaning with strawberries. I spent that night at the foot of Europe's largest mountain plateau, the Hardangervidda, in a village called Kinsarvik, where happy hikers sat outside a wooden pub drinking cold beers, and the sun didn't go down until long after eleven.

The next day started out much the same. I was on the Highway 55, following the north bank of the endless Sognefjorden, the longest and most famous fjord of all. Several times I had to stop and dive in to cool off. I studied the map. If I stuck to the Highway 55, I would soon be on the E6. The E6 went to Trondheim. In fact, it went all the way to Russia.

I was listening to Billie Holiday singing "There Is No Greater Love" on Jan Erik's tape when the Highway 55 left the north bank of the Sognefjorden to join the Lustrafjord. And when the Highway 55 morphed into the Sognefjellsvegen I rewound the tape and listened to it again, singing along, not paying a great deal of attention to the road. I didn't know that the Sognefjellsvegen is closed for most of the year, because of snow. I knew that the Jotunheimen National Park stood between me and the E6, but I didn't know that it consisted of 250 peaks that rise above more than 6,200 feet. Or that two of these peaks are Galdhøpiggen and Glittertind, also known as the two tallest mountains in Northern Europe. Or that after the road has climbed at a gradient of one in two for a little less than one mile, it officially becomes the highest mountain pass in Northern Europe.

The Sognefjellsvegen climbed and climbed and climbed. Gone were the clapboard houses and trestle tables groaning with strawberries. Gone was the Sognefjorden. Instead there was the unmistakable smell of burning rubber. I opened the window, hoping someone was burning a mattress in a nearby field. The sunshine had given way to a wet mist and the temperature outside had dropped about ten degrees. The temperature gauge on the dashboard, on the other hand, had risen about a hundred degrees. Come to think of it, that stuff coming out from under the hood looked more like smoke than fog. I turned the tape off. The road had narrowed to a small lane. It was a while before I found somewhere I could pull over, a lay-by overlooking a deep valley that kept disappearing behind thick, damp clouds.

I climbed down from the cab, opened the hood, and looked at the engine. Unfortunately I didn't know much about engines, although thanks to Ben I had learned where you put water in. I unscrewed the radiator cap and a jet of steam nearly took my eye out. There didn't seem to be much I could do until it cooled down, so I left the hood up and sat on the bed.

The silence was deafening.

I had finished all my books. I couldn't take a hot bath, or even a shower. I had nothing to smoke and nothing to drink. I had nothing to watch or listen to (I couldn't play tapes when I wasn't driving in case I drained the battery). In the end I pulled my cello out of the cupboard. There was just enough room to play it inside the van if I sat sideways, facing the cooker, and didn't do any long bow strokes.

When I woke in the morning the mist had gone. I poured water into the radiator and started the engine. I left the hood up and stared at it for a while. Everything looked normal. There was no smell of burning rubber. I climbed into the driver's seat and resumed my vertical ascent.

I made it to the top. To the point where the Sognefjellsvegen finally stops climbing and prepares to cross the Jotunheimen National Park. It was incredible. The road was a narrow strip of tarmac carved out of snowdrifts twelve feet high. Everything else was so white I could hardly tell which way was up anymore. To the east, rising out of the snow, were the jagged, ice-covered peaks of Glittertind and Galdhøpiggen. I felt a stab of longing to go further in, to hike all day like the people who were gathering with maps and boots and backpacks, and then drink beer in the sun and wash my tired feet in an ice-cold river. But the midnight sun wouldn't wait for me, and the diesel warning light was on. All that climbing had emptied my fuel tank. I consulted Aase's map. There was a small town called Lom on the other side of the Jotunheimen. I pulled out the biscuit tin and counted my money. I still had two hundred kroner. I prayed that Lom had a gas station.

Lom did have a gas station. Unfortunately, by the time I got there, it was closed. I decided to press on. There had to be another town soon.

There wasn't.

I was on the E6 and halfway across another national park, called the Dovrefjell, when the van spluttered, coughed, and died. I managed to roll off the road and onto a patch of dirt next to some deserted barns. The barns seemed to belong to the national park authority. On all the doors were big signs warning about musk oxen, which looked like overgrown sheep with long straggly fringes like aging rock stars and huge tusks like woolly mammoths. According to the signs musk oxen were vegetarian but neurotic. They wouldn't eat you, but they might accidentally gore you to death.

I made a cup of tea and sat by the road with it so I could flag down a car. Not that I had seen a car yet on the E6. I unpacked my cello and tried to work out how to play "There Is No Greater Love." Then I made another cup of tea. I had drunk four cups of tea and played "There Is No Greater Love" twelve times when a Land Rover finally appeared. I didn't have to flag it down in the end. It pulled over anyway. The man who got out was wearing khaki shorts.

"There is no parking here," he said, looking at my cello.

I cleared my throat.

"Actually I've run out of diesel."

The man hauled a rusty jerry can out of the back of the Land Rover.

"You're in luck," he said. "Where are you going?"

"Trondheim. Well, Nordkapp. But Trondheim first."

He splashed diesel liberally into my tank.

"I've only got two hundred kroner," I said, anxiously.

"You will need more than two hundred kroner to get to Nordkapp."

"I know that."

I picked up my cello and started packing it into the case.

"Why do you have a cello?"

"I am a busker," I said. "I play music on the street for money. That's how I'm going to get to Nordkapp."

"Then play for me and keep your two hundred kroner."

"Oh no. I don't mind paying."

"I would rather hear you play the cello. It's not often that I hear somebody playing the cello on the side of the E6. I love the *Bach Suites*."

Because of this I tried to play the Minuet, but I'd forgotten it, and halfway through it accidentally morphed into "There Is No Greater Love," then it came unstuck altogether and I stopped. I could feel myself blushing.

"That was awful," I said.

The man didn't disagree. He laughed and told me I could keep the diesel anyway, because it was the Norwegian equivalent of red diesel and I'd probably get arrested. I put the cello in the cupboard.

"I don't suppose you know where I can get any water."

"There is a river over there," he said.

"I mean drinking water."

"This isn't England. You can drink from the rivers in Norway."

Trondheim was a disaster, too.

There were so many buskers I thought I was seeing double. All of them were foreign, from distant corners of Europe, where kroner are worth sleeping on the street for. Tough-looking teenagers with battered guitars hissed and spat at me. Naked men in silver paint pretended to be statues. Other men in gold paint pretended to be birds. A girl who was definitely under ten played a mandolin and tried not to cry. To top it all off, a boy of about twelve sat on the edge of Torvet, the main square, and played the Haydn *Cello Concerto in C*. Not only that, but he had a pickup and was plugged into a portable amp. I pushed my way to the front of the crowd that had gathered around him and watched his fingers zipping up and down the strings like Yo-Yo Ma. He finished the first movement and went straight to the third and most difficult, missing out the melancholy adagio in the middle.

I went back to the van, put the cello in the cupboard, closed all the doors, lit a candle, and studied the guidebook. The guidebook said there were no towns worth mentioning until Mo i Rana, 310 miles away, on the edge of the Arctic Circle. Apart from a small and ugly place that grew up around a noisy rail junction on the far side of the Trondheimsfjorden. Called Hell.

I slept in Hell that night. Or rather, I slept just outside it, in a narrow lay-by right next to the busiest stretch of road I had come across since I left England. I was woken in the middle of the night by someone knocking on the side of the van. I sat up. They knocked again. I pulled on some clothes and peered through the hole in the bulkhead. Two policemen stood outside shining torches at my tires. I opened the door, trying not to think about the red diesel.

"What are you doing?"

They shone their torches into the van.

"Sleeping."

"You cannot sleep here."

They led me to a car park, where I lay wide awake through the rest of the long, light night.

Hell has to be the worst town in the world for busking. There are no squares. No cafés. Just freight trains and car parks and run-down shops with no customers. Eventually I set up right outside the freight depot, which was the only place with any people. I tried "Summertime" and "Autumn Leaves." Nothing. I tried Haydn and Bach. Nothing. I tried "There Is No Greater Love." Two men in greasy overalls walked over from the freight depot, laughed, and put twenty kroner in the hat. It was a start. Then the policemen I had met in the night arrived. There clearly wasn't much crime in Hell.

"You cannot play music here."

I was desperate.

"Not even for charity?"

"What charity?"

"Homeless people," I said, staring him straight in the eye. "And dead people."

The policemen took me to a shopping center I hadn't noticed because it looked more like a multi-story car park.

They persuaded the security guards to let me play inside it for three days. Which was just long enough for a tank of diesel and a postcard for Ben that had a picture of the freight depot with "Hell, God's Ekspedisjon" scrawled across it.

The journey from Hell to Mo i Rana took another two days and two nights. I didn't care. Quite the reverse. Away from the towns, driving was the easy bit. This time, instead of fjords, there were the wooded valleys of Trøndelag, eventually giving way to Nordland, which was wild and bleak and full of empty plateaus and endless snaking rivers. Even if I had been able to afford to stay in campsites I couldn't have done because there weren't any. There didn't need to be. With Trondheim and Hell 60 miles behind me, and Mo i Rana 310 miles in front of me, there was nobody to care about some yellow van driven a few hundred meters across the scrub from the E6 and parked with its back doors looking out over one of the endless snaking rivers. There was nobody to see it.

I practically lived in those rivers. I washed in them. I washed my clothes in them. I washed my hair in them. I did my washing up in them. I drank them. When they were vigorous I showered under powerful waterfalls. When they were lazy I lay naked in them as if they were a tepid bath. I listened to them as if they were music. I had no buzzing fridge, no fizzing lightbulbs, no gurgling pipes. There was no distant hum of traffic. There were no voices in the street. There were no streets. There was nothing, apart from the crackling of a candle flame and the voices in my head, the memories that wouldn't leave me alone, that pestered me like the whining of mosquitos.

Dead.

I wish I could feel you naked beside me.

Dead.

Nothing.

We could be troubadours.

I would have run from them, distracted myself in some way, called someone, drunk something, watched something on television, but all I could do was wait and hope they would fade. I sat on the back step of my old, rusting van and stared out at the mountains or the river or whatever that night's backdrop was, and gradually they did fade. The memories and the past they belonged to were swallowed up by the silence, like everything else. If I had known how lonely and remote those park-ups were going to be, I would have been gripped with terror at the thought of it, but it never got dark, and gradually I realized that I was not afraid.

Aside from the time I spent at Jan Erik's, I had survived for a month on milky coffee, porridge, pasta, rollmops, and grated carrots. I saved all the bigger coins for diesel, which meant that visiting supermarkets was a fraught experience involving fistfuls of coppers, which I would painstakingly count at the checkout while people piled up behind me. I didn't have much choice. I couldn't exactly go to a bank. I never knew quite how much I had, either, although I grew more and more skilled at guessing from the weight of the coins in my hands. When I was short by a few kroner the lady at the checkout would usually let me off, because she couldn't face the thought of counting all those coins again.

I reached Mo i Rana on 14 July. It's an old industrial town from which all the industry has long since departed. These days the streets are lined with benches, on which elderly ladies and gentlemen gathered to listen to me play my cello outside the Coop. Their favourite was "Autumn Leaves." Whenever I packed up they would ask me when I was coming back, as if I was a real musician. And they were generous, too. I busked twice a day, once in the morning and once in the afternoon, and it became a happy ritual to empty the pockets of my torn and faded jeans out onto the plywood offcut that served as my kitchen, and count my coins. One day I counted eight hundred kroner. Eighty pounds. It seemed nothing short of miraculous.

I could have stayed longer in Mo i Rana, but time was running out. It was already too late to see the midnight sun in Bodø, a few hundred kilometers further north. If I was lucky I might just make it to Tromsø. I left on a Sunday and traveled west to the Kystriksveien, a coastal route that passes close to the Svartisen glacier. Andrew had always wanted to see a glacier.

Part of the Kystriksveien is a sea ferry. I left my van in a queue of three, in a tiny harbor called Kilboghamn, and went to stand on the edge of a stone pier. The sea was slapping up against enormous tractor tires fifteen feet wide, indicators of how intense the winter storms must get up there. An icy wind was blowing. I went back to the van and changed my flip-flops for boots and socks and made a flask of tea. By the time I finished the ferry had arrived.

Up on deck I was alone. The other travelers sensibly sat inside, out of the wind, behind the salt-caked windows. I breathed wet, salty air and listened to the restless crying of gulls. Above me clouds raced across the sun. Rocks eroded by ice towered over the water, casting strange shadows. A handful of courageous trees clung to threadbare slopes. From here the land looked bald, as if it had been scoured with a Brillo pad. The wind caught the sea and whipped it into frothy waves.

A couple of fishing huts with their windows boarded up clung to the shoreline.

We passed a lone green buoy. There was a loud blast and a voice crackled into life over the loudspeaker.

"Ladies and gentlemen," it said, in Norwegian and then in English.

"Welcome to the Arctic Circle."

12

I busked in Bodø and then traveled east to Narvik, an industrial port that's only a city by Norwegian standards. The scene of bitter wrangling during World War II, it's not an aesthetically pleasing place. After three days sitting outside the shopping center trying to avoid eye contact with security, I was relieved to be back on the E6. Doubly so this time, because my next stop, in just 180 miles, was Tromsø. I imagined tree-lined streets and old stone buildings, pavement cafés and jazz musicians. I was nearing my goal. The long journey would soon be over.

I drove faster than usual that day, and the one after, reaching Tromsø on the evening of 22 July. Not a day too early. Crammed on to an island called Tromsøya, one of hundreds of islands and islets in an archipelago surrounded by deep and very Arctic-looking fjords, Tromsø is on the far side of a long and elegant bridge. Beside the bridge was one of the weirdest buildings I had ever seen—a kind of huge, white, triangular caterpillar. I later learned that it was a church, nicknamed the Arctic Cathedral. I found it extraordinarily beautiful. Behind the church was Tromsø's tallest mountain, the Tromsdalstinden, which had a dusting of snow even on 22 July. The church, the mountain, and the snow seemed to live up to my grand expectations. I was jubilant. I had made it in time to see the midnight sun. I was also closer to the North Pole than I was to my shed in the garden of Broadsands.

I crossed the bridge and drove up the main street, which was deserted. There were no old stone buildings. There was an old-looking pub, called the Ølhallen, with some old-looking men outside. But it was made of wood. There was a very prosaic Narvesen newsagent, with covered steps outside, that looked like a promising pitch. There was something called the Polaria, which seemed to be some kind of cross between a museum and an aquarium, with polar bears on the sign. There were some grocery stores: a Coop and a Rimi. A little bit further along there was a phone box. And that was it. I drove along the fjord and then spent an hour lost in the suburbs, looking for a place to park up for the night and watch the midnight sun. But there were too many houses crammed on to the tiny island, and the only places you could park seemed to be graveyards.

I stuck to the road nearest the water, which took me through a tunnel and along the north edge of the island. It was getting late. The jagged mountains on the other side of the water looked wild and untameable. They belonged to the Arctic of my imagination. There was a sharp wind blowing from the north, and although it wasn't cold, the wind on the fjord made it look cold. It felt like a place where humans were merely squatting, as if at any moment the whole city could be reclaimed by the wilderness that encircled it, the houses crushed by the weight of the mountains, the streets turned back into frozen fjords. Nothing could have been less like Paris.

Eventually I found a place to park. It was called Sydspissen, and it was at the end of a short dirt track on the corner of the island where south becomes west. There were no houses, apart from a crumbling yellow building that was covered in graffiti. There was a beach of sorts—at least, there were boulders that led to the edge of the cold-looking fjord. There were no vehicles, just a lone wooden canoe pulled up on its side, as if it had been abandoned.

I don't know what I was expecting. A welcoming committee, perhaps. Somebody to pat me on the back and say well done. Some Parisian-style bar, where I could treat myself to a glass of red wine and tell everyone about my great achievement. And what about the midnight sun? That thing I had come so far to see. Jan Erik's friend had definitely said you could see it from Tromsø, but I had driven all over the island and I hadn't found anywhere with a clear view of the sky. There were too many of those jagged mountains getting in the way.

I parked the van so the back doors were facing the mountains. I made a cup of tea and took it to the beach. I sat on one of the boulders with a blanket wrapped around my shoulders. And I waited for midnight. And midnight came and went, and it didn't get dark, but the sun was not bouncing around on the horizon, or if it was, I couldn't see it.

The next morning I left the van where it was and walked back to the main street along the Strandvegen, carrying my cello. It was a long walk, and by the time I reached the steps outside the newsagent my back was aching and I had a painful blister on my right toe where my flip-flop was rubbing. I unpacked my cello and tried to feel good. I had done it. I had busked my way to the midnight sun. It wasn't the way I had expected, but that was life. Things had never been the way I expected. Obviously the midnight sun was symbolic. It didn't really exist. It was a way of saying that it never got dark, and it hadn't got dark. I had forgotten what dark even looked like. I tried to count my blessings. There were no panpipes, the pitch was good, and once I had made enough money I could turn around and go home, and nobody would be able to say I told you so.

On my way back along the Strandvegen I stopped to buy an international phone card. I swam in the fjord, which was full of rocks and seaweed, but better than nothing, and changed out of my shorts and into my torn and faded jeans. They were covered in tiny pieces of seaweed from being washed in fjords. I walked back along the fjord until I reached the phone box near the Rimi. The blister was hurting so much I had to take my flip-flops off and walk barefoot.

Ben answered the phone.

"I've done it. I'm at the midnight sun."

"Fuck. You're never at Nordkapp?"

"No, Tromsø. But you can still see it here. Or you could last night." In theory anyway. "Tromsø is the Paris of the north, you know."

"Fuck."

"More like Penzance." I tried to laugh but actually I wanted to cry. I gripped the receiver. "Anyway, I'm coming home now. I can't wait. I can't wait to sit in the bar with you and drink Rattler and not have to worry about the van breaking down and how much diesel I'll need to get to the next town. The distances are massive. You've got no idea. There's one sign when you leave Trondheim. One road sign. And all it says is Narvik, nine hundred kilometers . . ."

I noticed that Ben was unusually quiet. My heart was crashing violently against my rib cage. I knew something was wrong.

"Are you okay?"

There was a horrible pause.

"Jack's back."

I let myself slide down the glass until I was sitting on the cold concrete floor. Thank God. Thank God. Thank God.

"Can I speak to him?" I mumbled incoherently.

Silence.

"Ben?"

"Christ, I shouldn't be the one . . ." said Ben.

"The one what?"

"He's got a fucking girl with him."

There were ants on the floor. Little red ones, bustling around like office workers.

"Are you still there?"

"A girl?" I said, eventually, in a voice I hardly recognized. "What kind of girl?"

"Sweet, I suppose. Petite."

I held the receiver at arm's length like it was a bomb about to detonate. But I could still hear him.

"Surfs," he was saying. "Wears technical trousers. Are you okay?"

I could hardly breathe.

"Where are they living?" I croaked.

But I already knew the answer.

"Um, in the shed. For now. Just until they find somewhere better."

"My shed?"

"Fuck. I mean, it's his shed really. He's the one . . ."

I dropped the phone. I leaned against the glass. I couldn't even cry.

Part Two:

The Midnight Sun

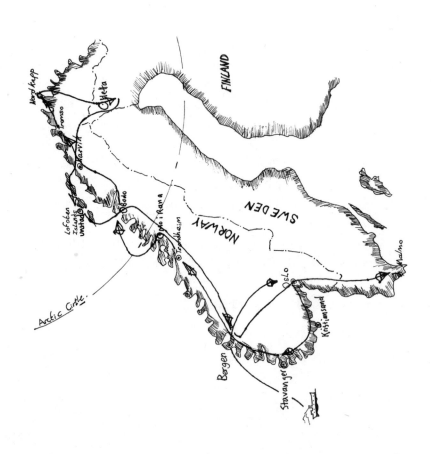

Nord Kapp

Tromso

Hetta

FINLAND

Narvik

Lofoten
Islands
Lunstad

Bodo

Mo i Rana

SWEDEN

NORWAY

Trondheim

Malmo

Arctic Circle

Oslo

Kristiansand

Bergen

Stavanger

13

Not crying didn't last long. It was as if someone had screwed a corkscrew into my chest and was slowly pulling out my heart with it. I cried all the way back to the van. I cried all night. I cried all the way back to the newsagent the next day. I cried while I busked, tears squeezing themselves out from under my closed eyes. I didn't care anymore. And I didn't play "Summertime," either. I stopped trying to be cheerful and dredged up the most tragic-sounding thing I knew; Rachmaninoff's "Vocalise." It's a beautiful piece of music and I love it with all my heart, but even I knew it was utterly unsuitable for a sunny summer's day in the Arctic. I played it anyway, over and over again, and to my great surprise people took to standing around in groups to listen. Sometimes they even applauded. They all gave me money. I was making more money from playing Rachmaninoff's "Vocalise" than I'd ever made in my whole life. At this rate I could be home in a couple of weeks.

Only there was no home anymore.

I cried in the Rimi supermarket where I bought cheap bottles of beer to drink on the bouldery beach, in the hope that it would knock me out. It never did. Instead I lay in bed for hours every night, watching a film on the inside of my eyelids of Jack and some sweet petite surfer in technical trousers having sex in our bed, and woke up with a crashing headache. I longed for darkness. But instead of darkness there was the bloody midnight sun shining on and on and on, like a bad joke.

I was still crying four days later when Henrik crossed the street and dropped a pair of yellow sunglasses in my hat. He was tall, and had laughing brown eyes and a suit with the shirt open at the collar. He waited until I stopped playing. I picked up the sunglasses.

"Try them," he said.

I put the sunglasses on and the street was transformed with what I can only describe as a kind of late afternoon, Californian haze. Not that I'd ever been to California.

"Thanks," I mumbled.

"No problem."

He carried on standing there, blocking me from the street.

"Um, do you mind moving?"

He didn't move. Instead, he said, "How would you like to make five hundred kroner in twenty minutes?"

Oh God.

"I think you play nice."

"Look . . ."

"And you look nice, too."

What was it about playing a cello? Did the curves remind all men of naked women, or was it the way you had to sit with your legs open to play it?

"Thanks."

Henrik smiled.

"But I'm not a prostitute."

Henrik held up a hand and shook his head.

"No, that is not what I mean. There is a bachelor party in the Ølhallen for my friend."

"Bachelor party?"

He clicked his fingers a few times.

"He is getting married."

"Stag night."

"Ja! Stag party. It will be very funny if you play your cello."

It sounded pretty funny. It sounded like the most horrible, laughable, embarrassing thing I'd ever heard of.

"Why not?" I said.

I didn't much care what happened anymore.

The Ølhallen is the oldest pub in the Arctic Circle. It's attached to the Mack brewery, which is where they make the Arctic beer I had drunk with Aase Gjerdrum all those weeks ago. There was a deathly hush when I entered. This was probably because the Ølhallen was empty, save for a couple of old men propping up the old wooden bar and a giant cardboard polar bear. It was also, I suspected, because I was the first female to walk through the door since 1794 when Tromsø received its municipal charter.

It wasn't empty for long. I barely had time to install myself in a dark corner before fifteen drunk and noisy Norsemen came crashing in and squashed themselves onto two tables right next to me. Luckily, within about five minutes nearly every single one of them had bought me a bottle of Arctic beer.

I downed one of the bottles and lined the others up on the floor. I tried to breathe. This was not busking. This was not a busy street full of people who might or might not hear a snatch of something and like it enough to throw me a coin. This was a pub full of men who had already paid me to play and were silently waiting for me to begin. In short, this was all of my worst nightmares rolled into one. This was a gig. I downed a second bottle of Arctic beer and closed my eyes.

"That was very nice," said Henrik an hour later, after I had put my cello away and squeezed myself onto the bench next to him.

"Really?"

I felt almost high on adrenaline. Or maybe it was relief. Or maybe it was Arctic beer.

"Yes, but you play for too long. You play for an hour. I say twenty minutes."

"Shit. Sorry."

"Now I must pay you more."

He put two more five-hundred-kroner notes down on the table.

"You've already given me five hundred!"

"Five hundred for twenty minutes. That was our deal."

He picked up the notes and tucked them into the pocket of my jeans himself. The equivalent of a hundred and fifty pounds. I tried not to notice his hand sliding over my stomach. The man on the other side of me introduced himself as Yoghurt.

"Summertime and the living is heasy," he warbled. "In winter we have underfloor heating in the streets, because otherwise we would die of cold."

"Crikey."

Yoghurt's ancestors were Sami nomads.

"You like the sunglasses?" said Henrik.

I'd forgotten all about the sunglasses. No wonder it was so dark in there. I pushed them on to my head. Everything looked crap again. I reached for my latest bottle of Arctic beer.

There are two types of people in this world. The type that is made for serious beer drinking and the type that isn't. I belong to the latter category. Six bottles was easily my personal best.

I reached for my seventh. After my seventh bottle I decided that Henrik was quite good-looking. Even though his shoulders were too narrow. His hand was stroking my knee.

"What are you doing in Tromsø?"

I tried to focus but my eyes kept crossing.

"It's a long story."

"Where are you staying?"

"I don't know."

The stags roared with laughter. I thought I might be sick. Henrik put both his hands on my shoulders and massaged them gently, digging his thumbs into the bits that were aching from where the case was too heavy.

"Perhaps you can join us later in chaos," he said, when he finally stopped.

Kaos was a nightclub on the Storgata, just behind the newsagent where I had been busking all week. It was full of couples groping each other and sticking their tongues down each other's throats. There was no sign of the stags. I bought a double rum and Coke for one hundred and twenty kroner (yes, twelve pounds for one double rum and Coke) and went outside with it to sit on a wall by the fjord. I was wearing the sunglasses. The pink mountains looked yellow and so did the blue fjord. Maybe if I never took them off and never sobered up I would slip into a parallel universe where everything was yellow and nothing hurt anymore.

I looked at the houses, the shops, the snogging couples, the lives that surrounded me, and I nearly choked on my rum and Coke. How did they do it? How did they get up, go to work, have babies and dinner parties, buy flat-screen televisions and gym memberships, when underneath everything was just this emptiness? This dreadful, blank, incomprehensible emptiness.

I had just finished the rum and Coke, and was contemplating going inside to buy another, when someone sat down next to me and slung an arm across my shoulders. It was Henrik. He wiped a tear off my cheek with his thumb.

"Why are you always crying?"

I cast around for an answer that didn't involve the messy, complicated truth.

"Bloody midnight sun," I muttered, eventually.

"Don't you like it?"

"It's crap," I said, waving an arm in what I thought was a westerly direction. "I can't believe I came all this way just to look at a normal day. I mean, it might be night, but it's just a normal day. At night."

I could see that Henrik was trying not to smile. I hated him.

"It's fucking crap."

"You need to go on to the fucking Tromsdalstinden."

He pointed to the tallest mountain, the one behind the white cathedral. He looked at his watch.

"But actually you are too late."

"I know. Thanks."

I could hear people shrieking behind me.

"If you want to see the midnight sun like that you must go to fucking Nordkapp."

"Fuck Nordkapp."

"Ja. It is very beautiful. There you see the fucking midnight sun over the Barents Sea."

"Like you said, it's too late."

Henrik checked his watch again.

"No. At Nordkapp you have two more fucking nights after this one."

"Fuck that."

"Actually you need to go to Knivskjellodden. It is before Nordkapp on the road but actually further north. Not many people know this. Ja. There is no road to Knivskjellodden. Just a hike that is about four hours."

"Have you been?"

"Ja. But it was misty. It is always misty. Fucking mist."

"Why do you keep saying fucking?"

"I am trying to learn the English swearwords."

I stood up.

"Fuck. Bugger. Fucking fuckety crap piss face."

"Fuck. Bugger. Fucking. Fuckty. Crapissfay," repeated Henrik.

He stood up, too. He grabbed my arm.

"Time to fucking dance."

The stags were lurching unsteadily around the club like zombies on speed. Henrik bought me another double rum and Coke and dragged me on to the dance floor. The DJ was playing Abba, but Henrik pulled me toward him and made me do a slow dance. Everyone else jumped around and bounced off the walls, knocking into things and smashing glasses and falling over. Eventually, thankfully, we were kicked out.

It was strange emerging from a dark, sweaty nightclub at three in the morning into the bright sunshine of the perpetual Arctic day. We walked in an unruly and drunken fashion along the fjord in the opposite direction to my van. Henrik picked a yellow rose, which smelled of England, and tucked it into my hair. I stumbled and he caught me and left his arm draped over my shoulder.

We fetched up in a penthouse at the top of a smart-looking apartment block near the bridge. The apartment belonged to a man called Knut, who went straight into the kitchen and brought out a tray of coffees and a bottle of whiskey that he said had cost two hundred pounds. Everyone shouted loudly in Viking.

"*Takk takk. Tusen takk.*"

Maybe we never really know ourselves until we've drunk the best part of a bottle of whiskey.

It's certainly true that I had never been so drunk in my life as I was that night. We finished the first bottle and started on another, and then another. By the time everyone had finally passed out in Knut's various bedrooms and left me and Henrik sitting side by side on a posh leather sofa, I could barely remember my own name, let alone the fact that I didn't go in for one-night stands with strangers. Henrik lifted my legs up and put them across his knee. Then he leaned over and started snogging me, and before I knew it I was snogging him right back, and when he moved his tongue downward to my nipples, instead of telling him not to I moaned with pleasure, and when he unzipped my jeans and pulled them off along with my knickers and spread my legs and groaned and stuck his tongue down there too I pushed against it, arching my back. He moved back up to my mouth. I fumbled with the buckle on his jeans. He stopped to take them off himself. I watched him.

"You have to go to Knivskjellodden," he said, as he finally lay on top of me on the floor.

"*What?*" I gasped.

"You can't travel all this way to see the midnight sun and not go to Knivskjellodden."

He pushed himself inside me, rendering me unable to answer.

"Fucking," said Henrik.

14

I left the apartment before anybody woke up. I can't say that I felt good in any way. But I wasn't crying anymore. When I finally made it back to the van and sobered up enough to read, I looked at Aase's map and saw that Henrik had been dead right. There was a place called Knivskjellodden that clearly stuck out further than Nordkapp. Both were on the end of an island called Magerøya. I put the map away and slept until the early evening, then I went for a swim in the fjord and counted my money. With what Henrik had given me I had close to three thousand kroner, about three hundred pounds. I sat on the bed for ages, trying to talk myself out of it. Eventually I gave up, took some acetaminophen, packed up the van, put on the yellow sunglasses, and drove around until I found a garage that was open. I filled the tank with diesel, and I bought two jerry cans and filled them, too. I bought a cheese sandwich and a big bottle of Coke for the journey. There would be no time to stop and sleep. I had less than twenty-four hours to drive the equivalent of Land's End to London on a single-track road full of potholes (according to Knut) that passed through only one town. I was apprehensive, to say the least.

To the east and north of Tromsø is a region called Finnmark, which is larger than Denmark but has a population of just 72,000. This makes it the largest and least populated region in one of the least populated countries on earth. To the south is Finland, to the east Russia, and to the north the Barents Sea, otherwise known as the Arctic Ocean. The most easterly town in Finnmark, a place called Vardø, is further east than St. Petersburg and Istanbul. It was Europe, but not as I knew it. It was Europe with bears and tepees and herds of reindeer with huge antlers, standing in the middle of the road and looking at me disdainfully when I tried to inch past them. Jan Erik did his national service in Finnmark. He said it went down to minus fifty in winter. He actually shuddered when he told me. Finnmark, like Tromsø, is part of the sub-Arctic, the region immediately south of the true Arctic. Depending on local climates, the sub-Arctic is usually defined as the bit between fifty and seventy degrees north. Knivskjellodden was seventy-one.

It was Yoghurt, the one with the Sami ancestors, who told me about an Act of Parliament that had been passed on exactly the same day I disembarked from the ferry in Bergen. The Finnmark Act transferred 46,000 square kilometers, about 95 per cent of the land in Finnmark, to the inhabitants of Finnmark, Yoghurt's Sami ancestors, to be managed by a board of elected directors. The Finnmark Act was set up to formalize the unwritten knowledge of borders and rights that lived, according to Yoghurt (who, like me, had drunk quite a bit of Knut's expensive whiskey), in the heart of every nomad. Except the land does not belong to the people, he said, eyes crossing. The people belong to the land.

I gazed at it through the windscreen. I felt as though I was looking at the road through a fisheye lens, watching it get smaller and smaller while the landscape around it got bigger and bigger. I could see what Yoghurt was getting at now. This was not a land of fences and boundaries and neat little hedgerows dividing it up. This was a different type of land.

After a place called Nordkjosbotn, where it connects with the road that goes to Tromsø, the E6 follows the edge of the coastal fjords in a northerly direction until it reaches a town called Alta. Even though I still had more than half a tank I stopped to fill up again in Alta. On the map it looked like pretty much the only town that side of Russia.

After Alta the road headed east over a plateau called the Finnmarksvidda, all of which is above the tree line. Day turned into night. Not that you'd know it, unless you'd grown used to the way the colors changed ever so slightly. I felt about six thousand years old. Or perhaps I didn't even exist. There was nothing to measure myself against. No settlements, vehicles, people, or trees. Just the road, carrying me onward. Just me and my yellow van rattling through the wilderness.

It was morning by the time I turned off the E6 and onto the E69 and began traveling north again, alongside the coves and inlets of the Porsangerfjorden. I stopped to make coffee and wash in the frigid water. Cut grass was laid out to dry on huge homemade driftwood racks. Old ladies in colorful clothes sold reindeer skins from trestle tables to the occasional loaded motor home heading the other way.

A man in a booth charged me three hundred kroner to cross over to Magerøya. The old ferry had recently been replaced by the deepest tunnel in Norway, he said, reaching two kilometers below sea level.

"Two kilometers?"

"Ja."

I survived the tunnel, plunging down below the sea and then grinding back up again. The tunnel was gray, and there was no light at the end of it. Instead, when I finally popped out onto the island, the fog was so thick I'd have been lucky to see my own finger if I stuck it out three inches in front of my face. The man in the booth had told me there was a car park at the start of the hike to Knivskjellodden. I crawled across the island at 30 mph, missed the car park, ended up at Nordkapp, and had to do a thirty-six-point turn to avoid another man in a booth, who was selling tickets for something that looked disturbingly like Land's End. I found the car park eventually. Not that you'd have ever known it was a car park. There were no cars for a start, just a small patch of gravel on the edge of the emptiness, which you couldn't actually see because of the fog. Maybe, I thought hopefully, this wasn't the right car park. I got out of the van, checked that my legs were still working, and hobbled over to a tiny notice board on a wooden stand. It was the right car park.

The notice board informed me that humans have been on Magerøya for some time. It said that the island is mentioned in the Viking sagas, although apparently the colonies of razorbill and other seabirds feature rather more prominently than people. The coastline is barren and windswept. The interior is tundra: lakes, marshes, and willow scrub. I remembered tundra from school geography lessons. As far as I could recall, it was associated with glaciers and desolation. It looked like there was a whole lot of tundra between that car park and the midnight sun.

There were big piles of stones to mark the path. Unfortunately, the fog was so thick I could only see them when I was already standing on them. I carried a small rucksack with some food and water and a spare jumper. My boots were not technical boots. Within minutes they were sopping wet and oozing mud from landing in bogs.

The path to Nordkapp is well trodden in summer, and probably the path to Knivskjellodden too, but although it was still a few days shy of August, summer was quite clearly over. I felt utterly alone. I imagined my own funeral. Cause of death: hypothermia and insanity brought on from walking in Arctic circles for three weeks. I supposed my body would be flown back to Broadsands, although I didn't know how, as I had no insurance. Maybe Ben and Jack would club together. Only the sweet, petite surfer would probably kick up a fuss, and Jack would say it was my fault anyway for not telling anyone where I was going. I realized, too late, that I should at least have left a note in the windshield of the van, explaining what I was up to, so that when it was still there in two weeks they would know where to look. The fog was getting to me. The fog and the fact that I hadn't slept in twenty-four hours, or spoken to anyone apart from the man in the booth since I left Knut's apartment two days ago.

I eventually reached the sea. I couldn't see it, but I could hear it, and I could smell it, and I was relieved to find myself on a rocky beach strewn with what looked like telegraph poles. The beach was at the bottom of a steepish slope. I fell over going down it and landed hard on the rocks at the bottom.

I picked myself up gingerly. This would not be a good time to break a leg. I carefully made my way over the boulders and telegraph poles to a headland on the far side of the beach. I hauled myself up onto it, grabbing handfuls of tufty grass, and made for something that looked like a flagpole stuck into a piece of wood about ten feet away. There was a gold plaque nailed to the piece of wood.

Knivskjellodden, it said, *71 degrees north*.

The most northerly point on mainland Europe.

15

I climbed to the top of the headland. The atmosphere was surreal. Reindeer with huge antlers loomed out of the fog, trailing tiny calves that stared at me with wide eyes as they picked their way through hundreds and hundreds of carefully built cairns, as if for centuries every single person who had hiked out to Knivskjellodden had felt bound to mark their existence with a pile of stones. I was no exception. I knelt down, selected some stones from the ground, and carefully built a cairn of my own. It seemed like the right thing to do. And when I had finished and I stood up again, I noticed that the fog had begun to lift. I could see the outline of the horizon, appearing and disappearing, and I stood and watched until the fog had dissolved completely, and I could actually see the sun.

I wish I could describe what everything looked like without the fog, but all I can find are clichés, and there was nothing clichéd about that landscape. The ocean had pressed itself to the earth, flat and still, as if it was holding its breath. The horizon was the usual band of gold and the sky right above it was the usual thick dark red of a sunset. But other parts of the same sky were light blue, shot with pink, like dawn. Nordkapp, the place I had dreamed of for so long, looked nothing like I imagined; instead it resembled a giant red alligator striking out for the North Pole. The sky was not full of stars, but the sun was bobbing around on the horizon, taking bow after bow like a pantomime actor who refuses to leave the stage. And it didn't leave. Instead, the band of gold, which had narrowed to a whisper, widened again, and the sun started rising before my eyes and the birds started up a crazy singing behind me and the sky lightened and it was day again. A fresh new perfect day popped straight out of the sunset.

I lay on the wet grass and stared up at unfeasibly fluffy pink clouds. Fleetingly, I was overcome by a sense of something I had never felt before. It was like the end of a long jazz solo, when the drums kick back in and everybody suddenly knows where they are again. I pressed my ear to the ground, and listened to the reindeer munching, and then I sat up and listened to the faint murmur of the flat sea, and then I found myself murmuring a quote by Kafka that I'd heard once and never forgotten, because it sounded so beautiful. It was about learning to be calm and quiet and alone, because when you are calm and quiet and alone for long enough, that's when you get to see the world properly: "It has no choice; it will roll in ecstasy at your feet."

And then I turned my face into the earth and I cried. Because I'd made it. Because the midnight sun was everything it was cracked up to be. But Andrew was still dead. And Andrew would always be dead. And he would never know I had actually busked my way to Nordkapp, and he would never know about

Jan Erik and Henrik and running out of diesel in the middle of the Dovrefjell. And I cried because I wanted to go home. And I cried because Jack was having sex with a sweet, petite surfer in my shed, and I cried because life was beautiful and I cried because life was a terrifying roller coaster that wouldn't stop and wouldn't let me off, even though I knew it was going to kill me in the end, and kill everyone I loved. And I cried because once people are dead, no matter how many of their crazy dreams you live out for them, they're not coming back.

Never.

Not ever.

Even though I could hear Andrew's voice, as clearly as if he were standing right there beside me.

"Hello?"

I let out a huge wail.

"Hello?" the voice said again.

I sat up.

"Hello?" the voice said a third time, only it didn't sound like Andrew anymore. It sounded like it belonged to the girl who was standing two feet away from me, holding a camera.

"I'm sorry. I didn't mean to surprise you. I'm Hanna."

Apart from her hair, which looked like she'd shaved it off herself with a cheap disposable razor and no access to a mirror, Hanna looked fairly normal. About my height, maybe a bit thinner, with a pretty face made beautiful by these huge, yellowy brown eyes. Like me, she wore jeans and a sweatshirt and carried a small backpack. But Hanna was not normal. Hanna was one of those people you meet once in a lifetime—so different from everybody else you're going to think I made her up. But I promise you I didn't.

One thing that made Hanna different was the fact that she was born on the Lofoten, a chain of islands north of Bodø and south of Tromsø. I'd heard people talk about the Lofoten, not just in Norway, but back in England before I left. Like the Isles of Scilly, it wasn't the kind of place you would expect someone to actually come from.

"Now I live in London."

She held up her camera; a heavy, expensive-looking one. In her other hand she was carrying a folded tripod.

"I am a photographer. That is why I came to Knivskjellodden. I am on a commission to photograph the midnight sun."

Other things that made Hanna different were the fact that she had twelve brothers and sisters and had done so much meditation she'd actually had a real *satori*. (I knew the word from Jack, who wanted one quite badly.) It meant she was enlightened. An actual enlightened being. Which may or may not have been why hanging around her was a bit like being on acid, only without the fear and without the acid.

But I'm going way too fast.

Being the only people for miles around, we hiked back over the tundra together. This time I could see it, a gorgeous landscape of clear blue lakes and bog cotton, flowers flailing in the wind like tiny white feathers hanging on for dear life to thin spindly sticks.

Hanna walked quickly, the heavy camera stuffed into her backpack and the tripod balanced on her shoulder, held casually in place by one slender hand. Neither of us said much at first. After we'd been walking for about two hours we stopped at one of the cairns to drink water and rest for a few minutes. Hanna asked why I had been crying. It was the same question

Henrik had asked, only I didn't give him a truthful answer. I suppose I knew he wouldn't understand, or perhaps I didn't trust him. Another thing that made Hanna different was the fact that I did trust her. Even then, when I had known her for two hours. Or maybe it was just a relief to talk, after all those days and weeks of silence.

Either way, once I started I couldn't seem to stop.

I told her about Andrew and the senseless way he died, and how thinking about it gave me vertigo, and how I had thought that busking to the midnight sun for him would make it different somehow, but it hadn't. If anything, it had made it worse. And I told her about Jack and how I used to carry his ropes to the bottom of the cliffs he used to climb, but was too scared to climb with him. And how I used to follow him down to the beach and sit for hours watching him surf, and it never occurred to me that I should try it, until I heard about the sweet, petite surfer, only there probably wouldn't be any point anyway, because I was too scared of everything, including waves. I told her about the long weeks busking north to Tromsø and how much I hated it at first. I told her about getting drunk and sleeping with Henrik and how he was the reason I was hiking across the tundra with her. And by the time I had finished we were back in the car park and I was leaning against the van, more tired than I had ever been in my life, my legs collapsing under me. And then I told her that now I had seen the midnight sun and it was all over, I had absolutely no idea what on earth I was going to do with the rest of my life. And Hanna just eased her backpack off her shoulders and smiled and said, "Perhaps you are going to wake up."

16

It was the first of many strange things Hanna was going to say during the short time we spent together. I can remember all of them perfectly and I turn them over in my head often, even now. And the funny thing is that they all seem to mean more over time. As if they were seeds that Hanna planted in my head that just keep on growing. I suppose that's what she intended.

Hanna hitched a ride to Nordkapp on the back of a motorbike that belonged to a Danish headmaster she met in Alta. She hitched a ride to Finland with me. I didn't mind. The only difference was going south and then west from Alta instead of west and then south. She wanted to go to a place called Pallas-Yllästunturi, which was, she told me, the third largest national park in Finnish Lapland. According to Hanna, Finnish Lapland was bigger than Scotland and Wales put together. She called it Europe's last great wilderness.

The drive was easy. The road was empty and Hanna knew the way. Not that there was much choice. As usual, it was north or south, occasionally east or west.

"You need a compass," she said. "In Scandinavia you do not need a map, just a compass."

Hanna took control of the tape player. She was very particular, ejecting the smooth jazz classics and fast-forwarding through three more tapes before she found a tune she liked. It was an old-sounding song sung in cracked Spanish, with a lush violin solo at the start and an infectious Latin rhythm. Hanna told me it was an old Cuban song called "Bruca Maniguá." She knew all the words and sang along. I tried to sing along too, but my Spanish was awful and I had no idea what I was singing. Hanna tried to explain the lyrics to me. It was all about going into the mountains and finding the answers there, she said. We were singing to the mountains, begging the mountains to show us how to be free.

Mountains, help me find the paths of freedom.

It was about surrender.

Hanna told me that the version we were listening to was sung by Ibrahim Ferrer, from the Buena Vista Social Club, but that the song was much older than that. It was written by a blind man called Arsenio Rodriguez in the 1930s. It was not the kind of thing I would have expected Jack to have.

"It's beautiful."

"You should learn it on your cello."

When I had to stop and sleep, Hanna slept, too—in her sleeping bag, under the van. I said she could share my bed but she refused, and there was no arguing.

"I would rather be outside."

I had the feeling that she would always rather be outside.

We were headed for a village that was called Enontekiö on the map, although Hanna called it Hetta, right in the middle of the national park. There was a hike she wanted to do.

The trail started at another village called Pallas. Pallas was sixty kilometers away and even smaller than Hetta. It crossed the mountains and finished up the other side of a huge lake called Ounasjarvi. I could see the lake glinting through the trees from the car park of something called the Fell Lapland Nature Center, where Hanna had told me to drop her off. I could see the bald, purple peaks of the fells too, rising up out of the forest like goose bumps. The forest was primeval, said Hanna, who was on her knees in the car park repacking her rucksack with the food she had just bought in Hetta's only shop. She stood up.

"Why don't you come with me?"

"On the hike?"

"Why not? It is only three days. We can sleep in wooden Lapp huts. It is very civilized."

It didn't sound it. It sounded crazy, even dangerous. If she'd been a man there's no way I'd have gone. But she wasn't a man, she was Hanna.

"You said you didn't know what to do with the rest of your life. Why not start with this?"

It was impossible to say no.

I wanted the van to be there waiting for me when we finally made it back to Hetta, so we left it parked at the Nature Center and hitched a lift to Pallas with some local fishermen. It took about an hour. It took another hour to reach the first peak, which was called Taivaskero. I was sweating. Hanna, on the other hand, looked like she'd just got out of bed after sleeping for twelve hours with a cucumber face pack resting gently on her eyes. By the time we reached the first hut, called Rithmaku,

I couldn't wait to sit down. The hut was a hexagonal Lapp hut with a stove in the center, a basket of logs next to it, and a hole in the roof for the smoke. Around the sides were slatted benches for sitting and sleeping on. A hundred yards away was a hand pump that drew drinking water out of the ground. Hanna found an axe, chopped one of the logs up to make kindling, and started a fire in the stove. I collected water, filled a saucepan, and set it on top of the stove to boil.

Afterward I sat on the doorstep and looked out at the vast spaces in every direction. Inside the hut Hanna sat cross-legged and perfectly still on the wooden floor. She didn't move when I came in, so I went back out and sat on the doorstep again. In its vast emptiness the landscape reminded me of Finnmark. Only I had seen Finnmark through a windscreen, from the safety of a road. Now there was no windscreen. I was in it. Swallowed up by it. There was nowhere to go.

Hanna eventually came and joined me on the doorstep.

"Do you do that often?" I asked.

"Yes."

"Is it hard?"

"No."

"It looks hard. You didn't move at all."

"You just sit."

"Why?"

"It helps."

"What with?"

"Everything."

"How long do you have to do it for?"

"That was just twenty minutes. But for three years I sat for five hours a day. That is when I had the *satori*."

"Five *hours*? Didn't you get bored?"

"It was very interesting."

"In what way?"

"I saw things as they really are."

"So how are things really?"

"I can show you if you like."

"How?"

"Close your eyes."

Nothing happened at first, apart from my head went wild with thinking, and the thoughts seemed like fish, darting about in a tank and banging their heads on the glass. But I kept my eyes closed, and as I waited for something to happen I became aware of my own breathing; my chest going up and down, my heart pumping steadily. And as I became aware of my breathing it slowed down, and the fish stopped darting around so maniacally and I noticed the tiredness in my legs and how good my shoulders felt now that I wasn't carrying the rucksack any more. In fact I felt very good altogether, now that there was space to think about it. Better, perhaps, than I had ever felt. Which was odd, but probably down to physical exhaustion and all the endorphins. I could hear the crying of the Kapustarinta, a type of golden plover with the most haunting call of any bird I have ever heard. It sounded more beautiful than music. In fact it *was* music; and so was the sound of water trickling through the mountains and the sound of the silence behind it and the sound of the wind. All part of some cosmic piece of music that made the hairs on my arms stand on end. Or at least something was making the hairs on my arms stand on end. I felt flooded with warmth and peace, and something else I had never known. Confidence, perhaps.

Trust. I knew without a shadow of a doubt that it was all going to be okay. In fact, it already *was* okay. And *I* was okay. And I didn't just know it with my head. I knew it *physically*. In my bones, under my skin, in my chest and head. It was like heat, a warmth spreading right through me from my toes to the top of my head. In fact it was so strong, this feeling of warmth, that I panicked. I opened my eyes. Everything even looked different, as if I was wearing Henrik's sunglasses, which I wasn't.

"Did you feel it?"

"What did you do?" I asked, and my voice came out all strange.

"I wrapped you up in light," said Hanna, as if it was the most normal thing in the world.

17

"Some people cannot take it," Hanna said later, as we sat on the floor of the hut, sharing the pasta, eating it straight out of the saucepan with forks. "It is too much energy."

"What happens?"

"One lady wet herself. On my sofa."

"Seriously?"

"Seriously. She was very embarrassed."

"I'm sure she was."

"She didn't come back."

"Do you do it often? Wrap people up in light?"

"No."

"Why me?"

"I suppose you were in the right place at the right time."

I put down my fork and sat back on my heels. "What happened to your hair?"

"You will laugh."

"I won't."

"I thought that bodhisattvas had to be ugly."

I'd heard Jack mention bodhisattvas, but I never quite knew what he was talking about. I suspect he didn't, either. I think his bodhisattvas came straight out of Kerouac's *The Dharma Bums*.

"What exactly is a bodhisattva?"

"Someone who works for the complete enlightenment of all living beings," she answered, matter-of-factly.

"Are you a bodhisattva?"

"Perhaps."

"Why did you decide to meditate five hours a day for three years?"

"Why did you drive from England to Knivskjellodden?"

"I told you. I had a broken heart."

"So did I."

"Over a man?"

It was hard to imagine. The more I looked at her, the more beautiful Hanna seemed, with a kind of beauty that was more than the sum of its parts. Her features were pretty, and she was slender and elegantly built, but that wasn't it. There was something about her that made you want to be as near to her as possible, because being near her felt so good. Hanna opened the stove and shoved another log in it. Hanna said the logs were delivered by park rangers, paid for by taxes.

"Because men were not the answer," she said, shutting the stove. "And neither were clothes or money or my nice apartment or my expensive jewelry or any of the things I was told would make me happy."

"What if a man *is* the answer?"

"He isn't," said Hanna.

The distance we covered the next day wasn't vast, about twenty kilometers, but the terrain was mountainous, the paths were rough, and Hanna didn't go in for resting much.

Mostly we walked in silence. Occasionally Hanna told me things she knew about the landscape. The names of trees and of birds, like the Kapustarinta, which looks like a chicken up close, and to stick to the path in the valleys, because the muskeg (a kind of soupy bog that's frozen in winter) can be 100 feet deep and drown you. There were bones to prove it, not human, thankfully, sticking up out of the mud. Ancient trees, their branches like ghostly sculptures, rose out of the gloom and stuck their fingers in my eyes.

When we finally reached the second hut I collapsed on a bench. Hanna made kindling, lit the stove, went outside to gather water, came back in and set a pan on to boil.

"How come you've got so much energy?"

She was kneeling by the stove, cutting something with a knife.

"I do not think," she said. "You are always thinking. I can see you, head down, thinking about this and that, watching your feet, screwing up your eyes. As if there are better things in your head than out here."

She came and stuck the knife in my face. There was a shrivelled piece of leather on the end of it.

"Eat!"

I took a bite and gagged. "What the fuck was that?"

"Reindeer."

"Gross."

"At least you noticed it. What are you thinking about anyway?"

"Love and death and how crap they both are."

Hanna burst out laughing. "Love is not crap."

"It's crap when it goes. When it's lost."

"Love is energy. It can never be lost."

"How can you say that?"

Maybe she'd never actually been in love.

"There's so much love you can find it wherever you go. There are always people waiting to love you. The world is full of beautiful men, for example. If someone goes from your life then there is always someone else to take their place. Only you won't notice because you will be so busy looking backward at the ones who have gone."

"You really believe that?"

"I experience it all the time."

"But you're beautiful. Much more beautiful than me."

"Not better or worse. Just different. I have a job, for example. I have to go back to London. You are free."

"Am I?"

"Of course."

At the end of the third day we arrived at Hannukuru. Hannukuru was the reason Hanna wanted to do the hike in the first place. Because Hannukuru had a sauna. And not just any old sauna. One of the oldest and most famous saunas in Finland, the country that invented them.

Finland gave us the word *sauna* and we've abused it ever since with our lukewarm leisure centers and swimming costumes and fake plastic coals. The first rule of a Finnish sauna is no swimming costumes. You have to be naked. The second is that it has to be so hot you think you're actually being cooked alive. So hot that you can feel your pores opening one by one, as if the sweat is washing you from the inside out, driving out all the rotten stuff that's got under your skin. The third is that the plunge pool has to be a frozen lake made from snowmelt and surrounded by fells you have just walked over for three days, without washing, or even changing your clothes, so that by the time you take them off they are sticking to you like a cold, damp flannel.

After the sauna we lit a fire outside. We were nearing the end of the trail. It was our last night together in the wilderness.

"What do you think about death?" I said when we had finished eating and were leaning back against the stump of a tree staring up at a lost star in the light blue sky.

"I think in some ways it is an illusion."

"What do you mean?"

"In the same way that we are illusions."

I sighed. It's the kind of thing Jack used to say when he'd upset me.

It's just an illusion, baby.

"But saying that we're illusions doesn't change the fact that people die and when they're gone we miss them and it's scary because we don't know where they've gone and we can't ask them what it's like and we don't know if they're unhappy or missing us."

"I think that those concepts are all illusions."

"I just don't get it."

"Death is life. Life is death. It is only words that make one good and the other bad. Actually they are the same. You could not have one without the other."

"But death is terrifying."

"If death is terrifying then life must also be terrifying."

"Life is terrifying."

"Then death will also be terrifying."

"Bruca Maniguá" was going round and round in the silence, like a stuck record. *Mountains, help me find the paths of freedom.* My head was spinning.

"So being alive is the same thing as being dead."

"Something like that. If we realize we're already dead, then there's nothing to fear."

"So being scared of life and trying to stay safe is stupid, because even though what we're scared of is death, we might as well *be* dead."

It was hard to think straight.

"In other words, living in fear is the same as being dead, because we spend all our time trying to be safe, and sitting inside and watching television and smoking joints and we don't actually *do* anything."

"Exactly," said Hanna.

I stared at the fire. "I'm still fucking scared of everything."

"You swear too much."

"I know."

"Fear is just fear. Don't take it too seriously. It doesn't matter."

"No. It does matter. I want to be like you. I don't want to be scared of everything. Like now.

"I'm scared of what lies ahead. I'm scared that when I get back to the van and say good-bye to you I will feel like I did before I met you. That nothing will have changed."

"Then you must find your key."

I had to stifle a giggle. I imagined an old, rusty key the size of my hand, and some old man with a gray beard dangling it in front of my face—*come and get it!*

"How exactly do I do that?"

"Think of something you really, truly want to do but don't because you are afraid. Not something you have to do or think you should do but something you want to do. Something you want to do with your whole heart. For me it was meditation. There was a group who met once a week and I used to go every time but I could not go in. I used to stand outside instead and watch them through the windows."

"I don't watch people meditating through windows."

"So what do you like to watch?"

"Jack."

"Doing what?"

"Everything. Climbing. Surfing. Surfing more than climbing, I suppose. The worst part of it all is the fact that she's a fucking *surfer*." I paused. "But even if I did want to do it myself, which I don't, because I'm too scared, I wouldn't know where to start. I wouldn't know how."

"You just do like you did when you got on the ferry to come to Norway. You take one step. That is all you ever have to do."

She stood up and fixed her strange eyes on me.

"And what matters in the end is not what happens but that you are awake, because life is short and these moments are all precious."

The trail ended the next day on the shores of the big lake I had seen through the trees from the Nature Center car park. The lake called Ounasjarvi. This time it was my van I could see glinting through the trees. There was a flag you had to hoist to signal that you wanted a boat to come and take you back to Hetta. We sat down to wait. The final hike had been an easy one, following a well-trodden path through the forest. I glanced sideways at Hanna. She had her legs crossed and was staring straight ahead. She had a ticket to fly from Hetta to Helsinki and from there to London, where a magazine was waiting for her photographs of the midnight sun. I knew that once we crossed the lake I would never see her again.

"I am not like normal people," she had said, that morning, as if I hadn't noticed.

She meant that, unlike Jan Erik, she wouldn't be giving me her telephone number. We wouldn't stay in touch via email. The wilderness was behind me. The midnight sun was behind me. Life stretched out again, empty like the road and with nothing at the end of it except death. I noticed that I didn't feel quite as daunted by this as I had done before the hike.

"What would you do now?" I asked Hanna, lying back and looking at the sky. "If you were me."

She thought about it for a moment.

"I think I would go to Unstad," she said.

"Where's that?"

"On the Lofoten."

"Hmmm."

"And I would stop wanting everything to be different all the time and instead I would live my life as if it was the best book I ever read."

I sat up and frowned.

"I wish I hadn't finished all my books."

Hanna opened her rucksack and began rummaging inside it. She pulled something out and passed it to me. It was a thick blue book written by someone called Tsoknyi Rinpoche.

"Don't you want it?" I asked.

"I have already read it. I think when you finish a book it is good to pass it on."

"Thank you."

She rummaged in her rucksack again. "I think you had better have these, also." She dropped two ribbons in my lap. One was gold and one was green.

"The ribbons are for fearlessness," she said.

18

I dropped Hanna off at Hetta's tiny airstrip. When she had gone I sat in the driver's seat and stared at the forest. I felt like I had been dreaming. Maybe I still was dreaming. Only I felt more awake than I had ever felt before. Hanna wouldn't say good-bye. It was the beginning of something, she said, not the end. And she was right about that, too. Although I never did see her again.

I climbed into the back of the van and opened Aase's map. It took me a while to find Unstad. It was hidden halfway down the west side of an island with a jagged coastline called Vestvågøy. I traced the coastline downward with my thumb, letting the exotic place names roll off my tongue. Strønstad, Sand, Delp, Laukvik, Sandsletta. I emptied the contents of my backpack on to the floor. I fished the ribbons out of the pile of wet clothes and held them in my hand for a moment. Then I leaned through the hole in the bulkhead and hung them carefully over the rearview mirror. I put a pot of coffee on the stove and picked up the book Hanna had given me. It was called *Fearless Simplicity*. I opened it at random. It was nearly as odd as Hanna. I flicked through it, reading sentences I only half understood, about being asleep and dreaming and then discovering that the dream is not real and waking up. I could relate to that, of course, but the book seemed to be saying that life itself was a dream from which we could wake up. The coffee was boiling over.

When I had dealt with the coffee I returned to the book, starting at the very beginning. Now it seemed to be all about freedom. About knowing within yourself how to be free, without needing other people to set you free. I thought about this. Jack had seemed free. I suppose I was envious of his freedom, of the way he could just up and leave like that, without caring what he left behind.

This book seemed to be saying that if you could find out within yourself how to be free you would not be needy any more. Hanna had said I was free. I sipped the coffee and stared at the mountains, which I could still see through the open door. Maybe I *was* free. It was a radical idea. I certainly hadn't been free before. I had needed Jack so much, clung on to him like a drowning child. I cringed. It was no wonder he had left.

I closed the book and poured the contents of the biscuit tin out on to the bed, stacking the coins into neat piles. There was still nearly one thousand five hundred kroner left of the money I had made in Tromsø. About one hundred and fifty pounds. I tried to work out distances. The only way to get to the Lofoten seemed to be a roundabout route through Narvik and then north to catch a ferry at a place called Melbu, then south again from Fiskebøl, the northernmost settlement on the northernmost island, which was called Austvågøya. It looked about a hundred kilometers from Fiskebøl to Unstad. I worked out that I had enough money to get there, but probably not enough to get back. I considered stopping in Narvik, like I had on the way up. But Narvik was a horrible place to busk. I decided to go straight to Unstad. I'd get back somehow. Perhaps that's what freedom meant. Knowing you'd get back somehow. I didn't want to waste any time. Unstad was my last connection with Hanna.

It was a long drive. There was a road that went west from Hetta to the border town of Kilpisjärvi, but it was unpaved and full of potholes. People were strung out along it, picking precious cloudberries in a bitter north wind. It was the first week of August but already it felt like October. I would have stopped in Kilpisjärvi to stock up on cheap food and diesel, but I had no euros and there was nowhere to change money. So I crossed the border and bought a tank of diesel in a garage just outside Narvik. The man behind the counter told me it had been eight degrees on the Lofoten that day.

It was six weeks since midsummer and the very heart of the night was dark again. There was something welcoming about the velvet darkness after all the endless light, but it didn't last long. Dawn had already broken by the time I reached Melbu at 2:00 a.m. Luckily the ferries ran all night. I slept in a chair in a bar that smelled of chips. After I disembarked I wound my window down so the cold air would keep me awake. I played "Bruca Maniguá" over and over again, rewinding and rewinding and rewinding the tape. The air smelled strongly of old fish. I later learned that this was the famous stockfish, the dried cod that makes the Lofoten economically viable.

Stockfish is such big business that trucks headed for Portugal and Italy travel with armed guards. A single fish can fetch a hundred euros.

I had planned to stop and sleep once I was on the islands, but I started driving south from Fiskebøl and found I couldn't stop. The sky was red and autumnal and the road hugged the coast, punctuated by dozens of tunnels and bridges. There were white clapboard houses and white sandy beaches on the seaward side and bare granite mountains to the east. Once I had skirted Svolvær, the main town, and crossed over on the bridge to Vestvågøy, the atmosphere changed again. It was wilder. The wooden hamlets were further apart and I was overtaken on dangerous corners by speeding cars, openly flouting the rules that were followed so carefully on the mainland.

The E10 curved inland and I nearly missed the road that went to Unstad. It was an interminable twisting lane built with oil money to replace the old mountain track that was closed half the year because of snow. There was no snow that morning. Just seagulls and chickens and a couple of goats tethered in a rough meadow by a lonely clapboard farmstead, and a gray mist and a dripping tunnel that finally spat me out to a view of the sea. The name Unstad translates as "no town," and there certainly was no town at the end of that lane. There was just another crumbling farm with a sign outside that said CAMPING, but no sign of any campers, and a line of rickety wooden fishing huts hung with broken nets that looked out over a rocky bay circled by mountains. I kept driving until I was about six feet away from the sea and couldn't go any further. I turned off the engine and stared at the sea. I couldn't work out why on earth Hanna had sent me there.

Until I realized that I wasn't alone, after all. There was somebody sitting out in the bay.

On a surfboard.

19

I turned the van around so the back doors were facing the sea, which was on the far side of a line of boulders. To my right the boulders gave way to a small, sandy beach that looked like it probably wouldn't be there when the tide came in. Beyond it was a long headland with a patch of very square woodland on it, so square I thought it must have been planted deliberately, perhaps for firewood. The fishing huts were on my left. A sandy track passed in front of my van, linking the beach to the fishing huts and the fishing huts to another wooden building that I thought must have once been a chapel, because it had a tower with a wooden cross nailed to it. In the field behind the chapel was an old bus with a car parked next to it.

I climbed out of the cab, put a pot of coffee on the stove, and sat watching the surfer. He caught a few short waves, and then he caught one and rode it all the way in to the beach. I had watched Jack and Andrew enough times to know that the surfer was good. And that the waves were not. They were wild and messy and breaking straight onto rocks.

I picked up Hanna's book, which said that the basic quality of illusion was bewilderment. I put it down. I cleaned my teeth. The tide was coming in. I sat cross-legged on the grass and tried not to keep looking at the bus. It had a stack of surfboards outside. There were more surfboards tied on to the roof of the car.

The surfer got out of the sea and walked up the beach toward me. He was tall and had a loose-limbed, loping kind of walk. I expected him to take the obvious route, the track along the shore that passed in front of my van, and I got ready to introduce myself. But instead of using the track he clambered awkwardly over a dry stone wall and crossed a couple of overgrown fields, wading through knee-high grass. When he finally got to the bus he peeled off his wetsuit, threw a bucket of water over his head, and disappeared inside. That's when I did something completely out of character. I followed him.

The bus was dilapidated up close. Even rustier than my van. The surfboards stacked outside were covered in snails. Grass had started growing over them. I knocked on the door, which was opened by a completely different man, who smiled and invited me in.

It was no ordinary bus. The line of windows facing the sea made the inside feel like a greenhouse. The line of windows on the other side had been boarded up. At one end there was a kitchen a bit like mine, made of sawn-off bits of plywood, and an ancient gas hob. At the other end were a couple of makeshift bunk beds. Aside from that there was a sofa facing the sea and a huge stack of old surfing magazines on the floor.

The surfer's name was Børge, pronounced Burger. His father came from Texas and his mother from Stavanger, although he sounded neither American nor Norwegian. When he spoke, which was not very often, he sounded Australian. Johan, who was staying in the bus with him, told me it was because Børge had gone out to Tasmania and stayed there for several years, building Viking ships. Børge wasn't much of a talker. He was more of a scowler.

Luckily, Johan was as friendly as Børge was sullen. In fact, they couldn't have been more different. Børge was tall. Two metres tall to be exact. Six foot six, with dark frizzy hair cut short. Johan was small and wiry, and had blond hair tied back into a ponytail. His eyes were brown and trusting, like reindeer eyes. Børge's eyes were slate blue and suspicious. Johan looked a little bit like Andrew. He seemed happy that I had turned up.

"The more the merrier."

Børge didn't look anything like anyone, and he didn't seem at all happy I had turned up.

"Who the hell told you about Unstad anyway?"

"A girl I met at Knivskjellodden," I said. "We went hiking in Finland. She's called Hanna. She was born on the Lofoten. In fact, maybe you even know her. She's got twelve brothers and sisters."

I suppose it did sound crazy. Børge shook his head in disgust. Johan promised to ask his Polish housemates. They knew everybody, he said, kindly.

Børge was sitting on the sofa. I sat down tentatively, as far away as I could from him. The sofa was so old the springs were poking through. The bus belonged to the farm that was also a campsite. Johan lived seventy kilometers away in a village called Moskenes, at the other end of the last island in the chain. But he knew the farmer at Unstad and sometimes gave surfing lessons to the campers. In return he got to use the bus when the surf was good.

"Unstad is the best wave for hundreds of miles," he said, grinning. "Actually it's the only wave for hundreds of miles."

"Bit of a curse," growled Børge, who had edged as far away from me as was humanly possible. Johan and I looked at him. "Now the whole frigging world wants to be a surfer."

Johan gave me a cup of instant coffee.

"You've timed it well," he said. "There's a big swell coming."

"Oh."

Awkward silence. I cleared my throat.

"Actually, the reason I came over is that I was wondering if I could borrow a surfboard."

"Sure," said Johan. "What kind of board do you normally ride?"

I wished so much I had been doing it for years.

"Um, well, actually I, um—I don't know."

Børge sighed heavily.

"I've never done it before."

I tried to maintain some kind of smile.

"You'll need a big one then."

Johan glanced at Børge.

"You got a wetsuit?"

"Oh shit, I forgot about that," I said. "Look, it doesn't matter."

"I've got a frigging board and wetsuit you can *have*," said Børge suddenly, getting up off the sofa and stomping outside. Johan looked like he was going to say something but he didn't. He just followed him. I went outside, too. Børge pulled a board out of the pile. It was pink, with a blue stripe. He threw it down on the ground by my feet. Then he went inside. I looked at Johan. He still didn't say anything. Børge came back a few minutes later and threw a wetsuit in my direction. It landed on my feet.

"I don't need it anymore," he said.

We both stared at him. Then he turned on his heel without saying another word, stalked off across the field, let himself into the chapel, and didn't come out again.

"Don't worry," said Johan. "It's not you." He shrugged and pointed at the wetsuit. "You'll need that if I'm going to teach you how to surf."

20

Johan's idea of teaching me how to surf was to bang loudly on the van at the crack of dawn as he ran past in his wetsuit, board under one arm, whooping.

"If you snooze you lose!" he shouted over his shoulder, when I opened the door in my pajamas and peered at him, rubbing my eyes. Børge was already out, miles out, beyond the seething shore break. To say it was stormy would be an understatement. The wind was howling. The beach was a mass of swirling foam. Behind it waves were breaking head high. At least the tide was out and they were breaking on sand, instead of rocks. The pink board with the blue stripe was lying on the grass right in front of me with the wetsuit face down on top of it like a casualty.

"Damn," I said to the gulls that were gathering, hoping for breakfast.

Mark Twain tried surfing once.

"I got the board placed right, and at the right moment, too," he wrote afterward, "but missed the connection myself. The board struck the shore in three-quarters of a second, without any cargo, and I struck the bottom about the same time, with a couple of barrels of water in me."

Which is pretty much how it was for me, too.

But first I had to get the wetsuit on, which took about half an hour, the wetsuit clearly having been made for a girl about half my size. I couldn't help wondering who she was. Børge's girlfriend? Ex-girlfriend? Maybe it brought up bad memories. Maybe that's why he had stalked off like that.

Once I was finally shrink-wrapped in black neoprene, looking about as attractive as a dog with rigor mortis, I picked up the board and staggered over the rocks with it to the beach. Little pieces of foam floated through the air like snowflakes. I tied the board to my ankle with the leash and waded into the water up to my knees. Johan paddled over.

"Try to get to your feet," he said, "and watch the rip."

Which was not very helpful at all.

I could see the rip. It was a current like a small river, where some of the energy from the waves was traveling back out to sea. Johan and Børge used it like a conveyor belt to take them out, behind where the waves were actually breaking. I was determined to stay right where my feet could still touch the bottom. Unfortunately, this was exactly where the waves were breaking. On my head.

"It's only water," said Johan, paddling over for a second time. "You look like you're waiting for a train to hit you."

"That's exactly how I bloody feel," I yelled after him as he paddled back out.

It's not that I wasn't used to the sea. I had grown up with the sea. It's just that I didn't usually go swimming in a fresh

143

storm with head-high waves, a massive rip, little pieces of foam floating through the air like snowflakes, and gale force winds. Nor would I normally attach myself by the ankle to eight feet of fiberglass. Watching a wall of water hurtling toward you while you are attached by the ankle to eight feet of fiberglass is exactly like waiting for a train to hit you. There is nowhere to go. When I tried to dive under them, like I would have done if I had been swimming, the board dragged me down and tried to drown me. When I tried to jump over them, it did its best to knock me out. And that was just dodging waves. Catching them was laughable. Even when there was a lull long enough for me to manage to get myself on to the board, I'd be knocked straight off again sideways, or headfirst, the board landing on top of me a few moments later.

I dragged myself out and sat on the beach. I hated the fucking sea. I wanted to peel off that disgusting wetsuit and dry myself with a towel and make a cup of tea and sit on a rock and drink it without being bashed around the head. I gazed longingly at the van. Damn that sweet, petite bloody surfer. And Hanna's bloody ribbons. And Børge, who was just waiting for me to give up. I forced myself back in. I wasn't going to catch any waves. I was in absolutely no doubt about that. But maybe I could at least learn to lie on the board and paddle.

I was so busy with this that I didn't notice I had drifted over into the rip until I was quite far out. The waves weren't breaking on my head anymore. In fact it was oddly calm. I struggled into a sitting position and looked around for Børge and Johan. But for some reason they were paddling away from me as fast as they could, out to sea. Then I understood why. It all happened so fast. The horizon went black and there was this eerie silence. Then the most enormous wave I had ever seen in my life thundered toward me. Børge and Johan just made it over before it broke. I didn't. It picked me up like a piece of driftwood and threw me headfirst over my board. My leash snapped. The wave played with me like a cat plays with a mouse it's about to eat. It tossed me this way and that, pulling my body in every direction at once, holding me under until I had no idea which way was up. I was panicking, gasping for breath, gagging on salty water and seaweed. Something grabbed my arm.

"What the hell are you doing?"

A pair of slate-blue eyes was glaring into mine. I spat water out of my mouth. I couldn't speak.

"Hold on to my ankles," said Børge.

I spent the rest of the day sitting on the floor of the van, trying to read Hanna's book, staring out to sea. My body felt stretched and shaken out. It wasn't a bad feeling, to tell you the truth, although I couldn't imagine I'd ever try surfing again. When evening came, Johan made a fire on the beach. I watched him from the van as he collected wood from the forest, brought it back, and stacked it in the middle of a circle of rocks. I watched him light the fire and then, when it was going, walk up the beach toward me.

"What are you doing?"

"Hiding."

"Why?"

"Didn't you hear? I nearly drowned. Børge had to rescue me."

"He said you handled it pretty well."

"What?"

"It's my fault. I should have told you not to go in today. Even I was shitting it when that set hit. Swell's dropping. Tomorrow'll be a different story."

I shook my head.

"I don't think I'm cut out for surfing."

It had been worse than Oslo. Worse even than getting stuck halfway up that cliff with Jack.

"I reckon you are. You're still alive, aren't you? Most people have to wait years for that kind of experience. You're lucky. You got it out of the way right off. Normal waves won't rattle you now. You'll get back in. Just don't listen to idiots like me."

"I'm not listening," I said.

But I was.

We walked together to the beach. I sat down on a boulder. Johan handed me a beer. Børge was standing with his back to us, his big frame silhouetted against the darkening sky. The air smelled of salt and there was a thin slice of moon overhead, although it was still light.

"That's the first moon I've seen for six weeks."

"How long have you been in Norway?"

"Since June."

"Why Norway?"

"Running away, I suppose."

"Didn't work for me," said Børge, bending down to split a big piece of wood.

Johan had to work hard to get me back in the sea, but he managed it. Mainly because the waves were a lot smaller the next day and the wind had dropped and the whole thing seemed a lot less terrifying. I think Johan felt responsible for my near-death experience, because he stayed in the shore break with me for ages, pushing me onto waves and showing me what I was supposed to do. I still couldn't do it. I didn't even come close. In fact, the more I tried, the more I realized that surfing was an utterly ridiculous activity. Like attempting to balance on a tin tray going over a waterfall. But the sun was out and when Johan finally paddled off to join Børge, I stayed in the shore break on my own, trying to stand up again and again until my body had that stretched, salty, wrung-out feeling that made me forget everything, even Jack, even the sweet, petite surfer. Or, if I didn't exactly forget, I was too tired and salty to care.

I quickly became an addict. As the week progressed it was as if all the salt water I swallowed every day was slowly washing the inside of my mind. The sea was like an anaesthetic. At night I fell easily into a deep, dreamless sleep. In the mornings I could hardly drink my coffee fast enough before I was squeezing myself back into the wetsuit for another fix. I stopped thinking about Jack. I stopped feeling sad about Andrew. I stopped thinking about anything at all, in fact, except my new and utterly engrossing relationship with waves and trying to ride them. I was hooked, in other words. Like a junkie.

The only thorn was Børge. He didn't get any easier. In the sea I sometimes caught him staring at me, and I imagined he was shaking his head in disgust. Presumably because I was part of the "curse" of everyone wanting to be a surfer. It's a measure of how addicted I was that I didn't let his attitude put me off. Johan made up for Børge's brooding silence in the evenings by the fire by talking at least twice as much as a normal person.

When I was neither in the sea or by the fire I tucked myself in amongst the rocks in front of the van and read Hanna's book. Even though it was easily the strangest book I had ever come across, far stranger than Jack's book of Japanese death poems, it was oddly comforting. I read it as slowly as possible. I didn't want to finish it.

Once Børge came and squatted next to me.

"I was just going to make tea," I said, nervously.

He nodded. I went to the van and boiled the kettle. I could see Børge outside on the rocks. He was flicking through the book, stopping every now and then to stare intently at it. His hair was like mine, frizzy and half dreadlocked from the sea. If he ever smiled he'd probably be quite good-looking. His body was okay anyway. Wide shoulders and long legs, like Jack, only taller. I set the red tin teapot and two mugs down on a rock.

Børge closed the book. "Where did you get this?"

"The same girl who told me about Unstad."

There was an awkward silence.

"What's Svolvær like?" I said at last.

"It's just a town. Nothing special."

"Is there a shopping center?"

"You want to go to a shopping center?"

"I need to get some money."

"There's a post office in Eggum," said Børge.

Eggum was the next village.

"I need to go busking," I said at last. "So I can buy diesel."

"Busking?"

"Playing music on the street."

"I know what it frigging is. What do you play?"

"Cello."

"You've got a cello in your van?"

It was true that I hadn't taken it out all week. I hadn't even thought about it all week. I remembered that I had wanted to learn "Bruca Maniguá." I poured out two cups of tea and handed one to Børge.

"That's a pretty cool way to fund a surf trip."

"Strictly speaking it's not a surf trip," I said. "Since I can't actually surf."

"Who cares," said Børge. "You can play the frigging cello."

I left Unstad and spent one night in Svolvær; a tiny, scrubbed-looking town hemmed in by the open sea to the south, fjords to the east and west, and mountains to the north. In the end I taught myself "Bruca Maniguá" right there on the street, remembering as much as I could and making the rest up as I went along. I couldn't get enough of it. Pieces of music are a bit like people. Sometimes you just fall in love with them for no particular reason. And I couldn't help noticing that the pieces of music I had fallen in love with were the ones that I ended up making the most money out of. "Vocalise" in Tromsø and now "Bruca Maniguá" in Svolvær. In two days I made over a hundred pounds, a thousand kroner, mainly from Spanish and Portuguese tourists who had come to see the place where baccalao is made. I couldn't wait to get back to Unstad and tell Børge. I spent half the money on a fresh tank of diesel, put some aside for a ferry, and blew the rest on cheese and wine and smoked salmon. Because right then it didn't seem to matter if it took me ten years to get back to Bergen. And because the smoked salmon was ridiculously cheap. The first thing I'd found that was cheaper in Norway than it was in England.

On the long drive back to Unstad I noticed once again how white the sand was on the beaches that ringed the mysterious-looking fjords and inlets, making them look almost tropical. And how fast people drove compared with the mainland, overtaking in a lawless fashion on blind corners. And how many bridges there were. Long, spindly bridges and short, fat bridges and elegant, white bridges like spiderwebs. And how away from the coast there was nothing but dense, rocky mountains, as if I was driving along the bottom of some giant, rugged boulder.

Navigating the endless twisting lane was like going home. When I popped out of the final tunnel I saw that Johan had already lit the fire. He was walking across the beach with a pack of beers. Børge was snapping wood against a rock. I put the van back exactly where it had been, opened the back doors, and watched the sea for a while. It was calm that night, calm and still. I could have stayed there forever. But storms were forecast, and Børge said that when they hit it would rain every day until Christmas.

I didn't believe him.

I should have.

21

The storms held off long enough for me to stand up and ride a wave all the way to the beach. A proper green wave, too, not just white water. I got to my knees first, and lumbered to a standing position about as ungracefully as possible, and once standing I wobbled a great deal, but I didn't fall off. Or at least, not until the wave had broken and I was on the beach in six inches of water. Johan whooped. The swell had dwindled to nothing. It was too small for him and Børge to bother getting in.

They held off long enough for me to read the final sentence in Hanna's book, which was about perseverance. And they held off long enough for us to climb the flat-topped mountain-like headland, south of the beach. They called it the Hammer. It was the biggest of all the mountains that circled the bay, with crumbling sides and a sheer cliff at the front that plunged straight down on to the boulders that stuck out of the sea below. I didn't want to climb it. I couldn't think of anything I'd rather do less.

"I hate climbing," I said.

"It's not climbing!" Johan hooted with laughter. "You could drive a car up there."

You couldn't.

"I'm going to stay and surf."

"There are no waves."

He was right. That day it really was flat. Like a millpond. Too flat even for me.

"The calm before the storm," said Børge, pointing to the thick black clouds that were stacking up on the horizon.

"Come on!" said Johan, jumping on my back and nearly pushing me over. "It's easy."

I glanced at Børge. His face was totally impassive, as usual.

"Fuck. Okay."

Johan was right. It was easy. Much easier than it looked. Not only that but all the way up we picked wild blueberries, stuffing handfuls of them into our mouths like starving children. At least Johan and I did. Børge didn't seem to like blueberries. When I got to the top he was sitting on a flat piece of rock, staring out to sea. Johan was nowhere to be seen. I sat on the flat piece of rock a few feet away from Børge. The view was outrageous. You could see for miles along the empty coastline in both directions and to the empty horizon, where the clouds were gathering.

"I don't want to ever leave."

"You will when it starts raining."

Since the day I arrived, when white flakes of foam floated through the air like a blizzard and I nearly drowned, the sun had shone pretty much constantly, even if it hadn't always been that warm.

"Unstad must like you," Johan had said. "It wants you to come back."

"Where will you go?" said Børge.

"Back to Bergen, I suppose." My mouth dried up. "Get a ferry to England." I felt sick.

"Why England?"

"I've been on the road for three months."

A cloud passed over the sun.

"So?"

"Can't bum around forever."

"Why not?"

I shrugged. "I don't know."

"If I were you, and I didn't have to go back to work, I'd bum around for long enough to spend the winter someplace warm that gets good waves, like Morocco or Portugal."

"What's your work?"

"I'm a mountain guide. In the French Alps."

"Is that where you live?"

"I guess."

It sounded like Børge felt sick at the thought of going home, too. Maybe his ex, the one whose surfboard I had, hated him and made his life a misery. Maybe she'd left him for a sophisticated and charming man, who liked blueberries and wore technical trousers. I wanted to ask him. I wanted to tell him that I knew exactly how he felt. Instead I said, "What happens to Unstad?"

Børge yawned.

"Fishermen come from Sweden, towing wooden huts, which they park on the frozen lake. Johan goes snowboarding in the morning and surfing in the afternoon. The tourists stay in Svolvær."

The sun was still shining when we got back to the beach, but the horizon had disappeared. Børge didn't like the look of it.

Johan drove to Eggum and called his Polish housemates. One of them worked for the tourist office. She said she could wangle me a free passage on the ferry to Bodø the following morning. Børge and Johan would go back to Moskenes.

We were all silent that night. The fire was smaller than usual because we'd used nearly all the wood and Johan couldn't be bothered to go and get any more, now that we were leaving. I leaned back against a rock and listened to the sea. I felt sad.

Sometime later Børge went to the bus and came back with something in a plastic bag. He chucked it at me. I took it out of the bag. It was a Patagonia duck down coat. Just like Jack's, only small and red and tailored for a woman. I held it up against myself.

"Try it on," said Børge.

It fit me perfectly. Whereas Jack's was huge and square, the sleeves hanging half a foot off the ends of my arms, this one could have been made for me. Børge's expression, as usual, was impossible to read.

"Are you giving this away?" I said, at last.

"No frigging way."

"Then what are you doing?"

I took it off. I wanted to ball it up and throw it at him.

"Patagonia send me clothes every year. I'm supposed to get photos of people in them for the catalogue. I thought it would look good on you. Especially if you were playing your cello."

"What do you do with the clothes when you've got the photos?"

Maybe he would sell it to me cheap.

"If the photo goes in the catalogue and I get paid I let the model keep it."

I put the coat on again. It was like arms, holding me close. I wanted it so much, I'd even play my cello in front of him. I stood up.

"I'll go and get it."

Børge shook his head.

"Can't do it here. It's a winter coat. We need snow. Maybe if you came to the Alps."

"The Alps are fucking miles away."

"So is Nordkapp."

"I haven't got a heater."

"You could borrow one. Park outside my house and run an electric heater."

"It would be too cold to busk."

"I could take you skiing. It wouldn't cost you anything. I've got plenty of gear."

Johan was oddly silent. I was dimly aware of him staring at Børge with a sort of shocked expression, like he had when Børge had given me the board and wetsuit.

We said good-bye on the quay at Moskenes, the village where Johan lived, which was right down near the southern tip of the islands, near a place called Å.

I gave Børge Hanna's book.

"I don't need it anymore," I said.

"Are you sure?"

"Yep. I've finished it."

I wasn't sure at all. I wanted to hang on to everything Hanna had ever said or done or given to me for dear life, but Hanna had said you should pass books on when you finish them and Børge had given me a surfboard and wetsuit, so it seemed only right that I should give him something in exchange. He seemed really pleased, and actually kissed me, on the cheek, brushing my lips with stubble.

"I'll return it one day."

I didn't see how. We hadn't even exchanged emails.

22

I made it back to the mainland just in time. That night the tail end of Hurricane Katrina caught up with the tail end of the Norwegian summer, with disastrous results for busking.

For the next three weeks my namesake trailed me like a stalker. She kept me awake at night, hammering on the fiberglass roof. She rocked my bed violently from side to side until I sat up terrified, certain the whole thing was about to tip over and bury me under three and a half tons of twisted metal. The van smelled like an old pair of sneakers. Washing was a distant memory. My shoes, my clothes, even my bed was wet. I got a stinking cold from sitting half under dripping doorways for hours on end, getting myself wet so that my cello would stay dry. If only I still had Henrik's crisp five-hundred-kroner notes.

The sky was so dark I had to have candles lit all the time. All I could do when I wasn't busking was lie on the damp bed and stare at the mould on the fiberglass ceiling and try not to think about the deep hot baths Jack and I used to share at Broadsands. If it hadn't been for the ribbons hanging from the rearview mirror and Børge's surfboard tied to the tongue and groove with bungee cords and the wetsuit hanging from the back doors on an old coat hanger I would have seriously doubted that either Hanna or Unstad ever happened.

It took weeks, that journey back to Bergen, and it left me drained and depressed. I finally got there on 30 September. I went straight to the ferry port to find out how much I'd have to save for a ticket back to England. Sweet, petite surfer or no sweet, petite surfer, I'd had enough.

Only I was too late.

The crossing had been canceled.

Ferries didn't go to England from Norway anymore.

Part Three:

Paths of Freedom

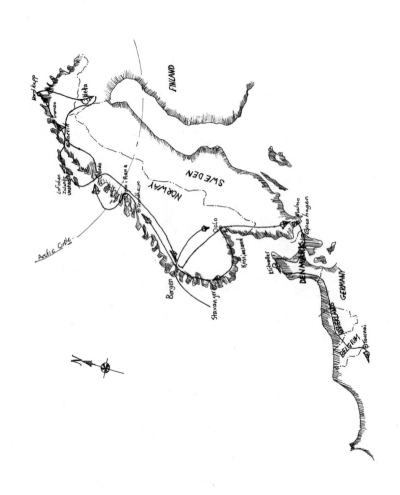

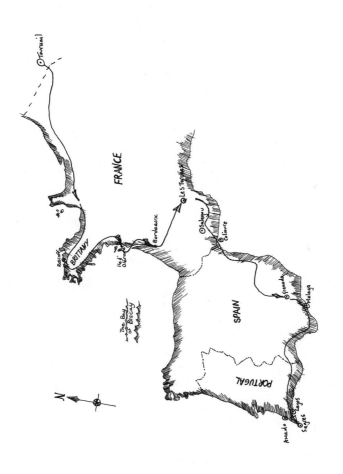

23

The rest of Europe loomed as strange and unforgiving as death. I had forgotten that when I arrived in Norway it also loomed as strange and unforgiving as death. Now, Norway seemed positively cosy. I gazed at the map in *Europe on a Shoestring*, at all the countries that suddenly stood between me and home. Sweden, Denmark, Germany, Holland, Belgium, France. The only one I'd ever been to was France. I counted the miles and worked out that the distance from Bergen to Calais was more than going to Nordkapp all over again. I threw *Europe on a Shoestring* on the floor and lay on the bed staring at the ceiling. If only I hadn't given Hanna's book to Børge. If only I was safe and warm in the bar at the hostel, drinking Rattler and impressing everyone, especially Jack, with tales of my brave adventures. If only the adventures were over.

The trouble with Sweden was that their biggest coin was worth only ten kroner, half as much as Norway's biggest coin, which was worth twenty kroner. This meant that as soon as I crossed the border my earnings went down by 50 percent. I had to play in every town I passed. I've forgotten most of their names. I remember that the rain stopped and that the nights were dark. I remember playing "Bruca Maniguá" until my fingers were cracked and sore. I remember swimming off the Skåne peninsula in freezing water and watching the stars come out one by one from the back step of the van. I remember the market in Varberg and I remember that I bought a cheap pair of slippers, because all I had were flip-flops and hiking boots with holes in them. It was almost October, and my feet were cold.

I remember the long, white bridge from Malmö to Copenhagen, and the big, green police vans parked in a line outside Freetown Christiania. I remember trying to navigate the many lanes of traffic and spending the night in the grounds of a mental hospital on the outskirts of Roskilde. I remember playing "Autumn Leaves" on Roskilde high street and walking back to the van past replica Viking ships that made me think of Børge. On the surface, nothing much had changed. I still hated setting up in a new town and breaking the silence of a busy street. Even though I still couldn't stand the thought of Jack and the sweet, petite surfer, I had still had enough. I was still going home.

But something had changed. I was haunted by thoughts of Jack, but I was also haunted by other things, new things. I was haunted by the wide open spaces I had left behind, and I was haunted by the sea. I couldn't stop thinking about Unstad, and instead of watching a film of Jack on the inside of my eyelids, I sent myself to sleep at night trying to catch imaginary waves.

I first noticed this change when I left Roskilde, having managed to save a hundred euros. Instead of driving west, toward Germany and home, I began driving north, in order to do a lap of Jutland before I left the country. I told myself it was because Aarhus, a university town on the east side of Jutland, would be a good place to busk. It was quite good, but that wasn't the reason I was there. I was there because Johan had mentioned that you could surf in Jutland. It didn't matter that I'd barely learned to stand up. My life was already folding itself quietly around my need to find waves.

After Aarhus I busked on the tiny main street in Skagen, which had almost certainly never seen a cello before, but which had spawned its own school of artists. I went to look at the place they had mostly painted, a long beach that directly faces Kristiansand, the town I fled to after failing to busk in Oslo. I spent the night in a big car park, empty apart from one other van. I woke early and walked along the sun-drenched beach to the place where two seas, the Kattegat and the Skagerrak, meet in a violent tidal race.

The owners of the other van came and introduced themselves as I was eating breakfast on the back step. They had seen my surfboard. They had just come from a place called Klitmøller, on the west coast. They said the waves had been good.

Klitmøller was an overgrown fishing village with several sandy car parks nestled in behind high dunes, the other side of which was a long beach. The sea was so flat that the two surf shops on the main street looked laughably out of place. I parked the van in the car park at the furthest end of the village. It was already home to a group of German surfers who were amusing themselves by playing competitive and complicated games involving tin cans and tennis balls. They invited me to join in, but I have never been much good at competitive and complicated games involving tennis balls, so I got my cello out of its cupboard instead, and hauled it up on to the top of one of several weird, graffiti-covered concrete bunkers that were half buried in the sand. They were left over from World War II and most of them were tilting drunkenly.

The sea was flat for three days. I stuck around, waiting, hoping. In order to avoid playing competitive and complicated games with German surfers, I took to walking on the beach and in the forest that backed on to it. It was a deep, dark, creepy forest full of pine trees that were good to climb and secret paths and clearings and shooting ranges that were used by the army.

One evening I clambered on to the flattest bunker with my cello and played "Vocalise" to a dramatic and beautiful sunset. That was how I met Karen.

Karen lived with her tiny daughter in a house on the edge of the forest. She had built the house herself, mixing the concrete for the foundations, wheeling it around in a wheelbarrow, building the walls, cutting down trees from the forest to make the roof, plumbing in her own toilet. She had learned these skills working on building sites to save money for extensive surf trips that she had made in a bright green Iveco Daily van with six tires and an old plywood offcut that served as a kitchen. Karen knew all about life on the road. She clapped when I finished "Vocalise" and then offered me a hot shower and the use of her washing machine.

It was the first time my clothes had been washed in anything other than a river or seawater for four months. We drank beer in her garden. Karen told me about all the places she had been in her Iveco, which was just like mine, and I told her I was heading back to Calais in order to catch a ferry home. She insisted on giving me a tatty old *Stormrider* surf guide, which was like *Europe on a Shoestring*, only instead of telling you how campervans couldn't overnight in lay-bys ever, or how much money was worth, it told you if a place had a wave and what kind of wave it was. Klitmøller was in there (rarely, not very good). Unstad was not in there.

I went to my van and found the map Aase had given me, so I could show Karen where Unstad was.

"You are lucky," she said. "Doing something you love as your job."

I hadn't thought about it like that.

"I love playing the cello, but I hate busking."

"Don't you like it when people give you money?"

I thought about the elderly people who had gathered on the bench to listen to me when I played outside the Coop in Mo i Rana. I often thought about them. In fact, it wasn't wholly true anymore that I hated busking. There were some things about it that I had grown to like. Mainly the feeling I had after a good session, the sense of achievement, dropping the coins into the biscuit tin and knowing that I earned them. I really earned them.

"I suppose it has its moments."

Karen picked up the *Stormrider* surf guide and began circling places that would be good for me, easy places, places for learning, with a big red marker pen.

"The Ile d'Oléron is perfect," she said. "It is warm and has nice waves and nice people."

"It's practically in Bordeaux!" I said. "I'm only going as far as Calais."

"Why don't you busk your way down the coast to Spain? Then you could go to Portugal. You could go anywhere. You are free."

I shook my head. She sounded like Hanna. And Andrew.

I stayed in Klitmøller long enough to spend a day trying to ride some small, crap waves that finally turned up and broke on the beach behind the car park. Afterward I went to a party at Karen's house, held to mark the end of summer. All the other guests were either fishermen or surfers, and they all brought huge bags of shellfish they had caught that day in Klitmøller. After we had eaten, Karen asked me to play my cello. I didn't let myself even think about it. I just went to the van, pulled it out of its cupboard, tuned up, found a chair and played "Bruca Maniguá." Then I played "Autumn Leaves." When I finished everybody clapped and carried on eating shellfish, and although I was shaking slightly I didn't let it show. I went back to the van and put the cello away. I was glad that I had something to offer. The fishermen brought fish, I brought music. That was the way it worked.

24

Civilization closed in after Denmark, hoovering up the wide, open spaces and turning them into endless suburbs. I've lost count of the nameless streets and cities I tried to entertain with the music I had taught myself in Norway. The further south I traveled the harder it all became: busking, finding places to sleep, finding places to wash, finding water. The nights grew longer and darker. Forests were full of used condoms and missing persons posters. Lakes were man-made and there was NO SWIMMING. I dreamed of Jack and surfing in equal measure. Once I even dreamed of Børge. We were sitting on the doorstep at Rithmaku, the hut where Hanna wrapped me up in light, and he was actually smiling.

I learned that some of the service stations had secret showers and I learned how to convince the person in charge to let me have the key. More often there was no key and it was a case of going dirty or risking a hairy truck driver walking in on me naked. Usually I went dirty. If somebody on the street expressed an interest in my music, which they did from time to time, I asked them if I could come to their house and take a shower. Usually they said yes. I started buying water in five-liter plastic bottles. Roads were complex and spaghetti-like, with endless opportunities for wasting copious amounts of diesel driving around industrial cul-de-sacs. The cities I ended up playing in were so big I often forgot where I'd left my van and had to spend hours searching for it, growing more and more certain it had been towed away and crushed.

All the countries had different rules, which I had to learn quickly, on the hop, usually by breaking them and getting told off. In Germany you could play in the big shopping center in the middle of town, but only for twenty minutes, in a specially designated spot, on rotation with other buskers. There was strict timekeeping and I stood out like a sore thumb. All the other buskers in Germany, at least the ones I met, were proper music students and played proper music. Not made-up versions of "Bruca Maniguá." On the positive side, the towns weren't hundreds of miles apart and I could move on quickly, and at least in Germany it was easy to find places to sleep. This was the spiritual home of the motorhome, and there were special areas set aside where you could park for free. I stood out like a sore thumb in those, too.

Holland was a different story. I'm sure it would seem normal now, but fetching up in Holland after months in Norway felt like fetching up on Mars. Not only were there no wide open spaces, there were no spaces at all. I felt like an ant, tunneling through an endless town on an endless motorway, surrounded on all sides by other ants. Fighting my way into a town was no easy feat, given the rivers of people flowing in all directions; finding a pitch was about being somewhere where my cello would have the most visual impact, and not getting trampled. There was absolutely no danger of being heard. There was plenty of competition, but it wasn't like Germany. In Holland the buskers were ravers, sitting wan and exhausted on blankets, smoking and playing didgeridoos, and the problem was not to do with rules, or that anyone had a problem with buskers, the problem was that, half the time, instead of money I'd get little packages of weed thrown into my hat, which wasn't going to get me home or feed me. Also, I had to spend some time taping it to the inside of the tongue and groove before I crossed the border into Belgium, just in case.

I had discovered two things in Holland, neither of them particularly encouraging. One was that you needed a licence to busk in Belgium, and that if you were caught busking without one the fine was a hundred euros. The other was that there was no money whatsoever to be made in France.

I'll never know if the first was true. All I can say is that I tried very hard not to busk in Belgium, but in the end I had to, at a town near the French border called Tournai. I did see two policemen, but I closed my eyes and carried on playing, and I kept them closed for twenty minutes, and when I opened them again the policemen had gone and there were twenty people standing around, who clapped when I finished playing "Bruca Maniguá" for the fifth time.

It was the end of October when I finally crossed the border into France, two full months since I left Unstad. It was only 60 miles from Tournai to Calais. The long drive south was over. Or at least, it should have been.

I longed for Broadsands, for Ben's grumpy humor, for the feeling of safety, for being able to wake up in the morning and not have to think about where I was going to busk that day, for not needing to worry about the van breaking down or being moved on by policemen in the dead of night. But now that I was so close to making it a reality, facing Jack and the sweet, petite surfer seemed more and more unbearable. When I arrived in Bergen, even after all the storms, I had been full of Knivskjellodden and Unstad and Hanna. Now, after two months of struggling through countless cities and sleeping in motorway service stations, all that felt a million miles away. I was pale and spotty. I hadn't been eating or sleeping properly. I lay on the bed and flicked through Karen's *Stormrider* surf guide. I picked up *Europe on a Shoestring*.

I didn't exactly plan it. I just didn't go to Calais. Instead I found myself in Dieppe. In Dieppe I discovered that the second part of the information I had been given in Holland was true. French people were not generous toward buskers. Which meant that I didn't have enough for a ferry from Le Havre, and as it wasn't a place I wanted to hang out, I carried on to Caen, and I still didn't have enough in Caen, and the police moved me on, so I carried on to Rennes. And I made some money in Rennes, but it was a big place and I couldn't find anywhere to park for the night, so I carried on to Saint-Brieuc, where I managed to save about a hundred euros over four days, and then I went to Roscoff, because you could get a ferry from Roscoff to Plymouth, only the ferry from Roscoff was two hundred euros, so I drove down the coast, ostensibly looking for somewhere to busk, but actually, if I'm honest, looking for waves that I could practice on—so I wouldn't make a fool of myself in front of the sweet, petite surfer—and beaches where

I could get a tan so I didn't have to face her looking spotty and pale and exhausted.

But there were no such waves or beaches in Brittany that week. Instead there were storms like I hadn't seen since Katrina hit Norway. So I carried on south until the sun came out and my money ran out, by which time I was in La Rochelle. I busked in La Rochelle until I had another hundred euros, and then I looked at the *Stormrider* surf guide, and I saw that the Ile d'Oléron, which Karen had circled with her big red marker pen, was just around the corner.

25

The bridge to Oléron was free, and the first beach I found was long and sandy. It was called Vert Bois, presumably because of the tall pine trees that backed on to the dunes. I parked my van next to an old white Transit with a "Creatures of Leisure" sticker in the window and three distinctly un-pedigree dogs lying on the front seats, tongues hanging out. They stood up and wagged their tails at me. The wetsuit felt as uncomfortable as it had that first day at Unstad. I carried the board awkwardly to the end of the sandy road, down a couple of steps, and across the beach.

After Unstad, the sea seemed to be full of surfers, although in reality there were only about half a dozen. I experienced a moment of acute anxiety and embarrassment. I wanted to get in quite badly, to feel the water on my face and go underneath the surface and get washed up like clothes in a washing machine. I needed that feeling of wrung-out saltiness. But I didn't want to fall off in front of all these people. The wrung-out saltiness won and I began wading in. The magic still worked. For three hours I thought about nothing apart from the weirdly fascinating and endlessly frustrating process of trying to stand up on moving water.

When I finally got out, most of the other surfers had got out, too. They were clustered around the Transit in the car park. The dogs came over first, tails wagging, licking my hands. I peeled off my wetsuit and hung it over the wing mirror to dry.

The next to say hello was Xavier. He came to get the dogs and didn't leave; pretty soon the other four had followed him and I had put the kettle on and someone went to get some extra mugs from the Transit and we were all sitting outside on the grass drinking tea. Everyone had wet hair and was salted and happy apart from the one called Jean, who had broken his leg falling off a footpath and wouldn't be able to walk, let alone surf, for six months. Jean was from Paris and the others took the piss out of his accent, which was, apparently, straight out of the film *La Haine*. Xavier was the extrovert of the bunch, cracking jokes constantly. Nadine taught yoga in La Rochelle. Étienne was a Breton. He had dark curly hair and an old white Transporter that smelled like a fish and chip shop because he ran it on recycled vegetable oil. Benoit was a professional skateboarder who said everything three times, *"Bien bien bien, voilá voilá voilá."*

The dogs were called Cash, Magic, and Silence. They belonged to everybody.

They all lived on a secret piece of land called simply "le Terrain." By the time we had finished our cups of tea they had invited me to stay there with them since the gendarmes didn't like vans at Vert Bois anymore, now that the right-wing Jean-Marie Le Pen was so popular. Xavier practically spat his name on to the dusty ground. They piled into the white Transit with the dogs and I followed behind. It was hot enough that I was wearing only my bikini, despite it being almost November.

Le Terrain was a few miles inland, at the end of a dirt track that burrowed through dense undergrowth that scraped the paintwork on both our vans, like fingernails on a blackboard. We reached a clearing. Étienne's Transporter was parked next to an old Renault. Xavier tucked the Transit in next to the Renault and signaled for me to go alongside. I climbed through the bulkhead, pulled on my torn and faded jeans, which had completely gone at the knees, and hung my wetsuit on a tree to dry, like the others had. The air was heavy with the smell of pine and tamarisk trees. There was a fire pit in the middle of the clearing and surfboards were heaped up like debris around the edges. The late-afternoon October sun was filtering through the trees like a kaleidoscope. There was a shabby-looking wooden chalet with a small veranda and a couple of tents. A sign hanging off a massive evergreen oak read "No Hunting on Pain of Death."

The land belonged to Xavier's uncle. They weren't supposed to be living there in vans because it was a nature reserve, but the only house anywhere near it belonged to a Parisian politician who hardly ever came to the island. When he did he liked to walk around naked and have sex in the garden with his gay lover, so he didn't want to call the gendarmes, either.

Oléron is France's biggest island after Corsica. According to Xavier, it gets more sunshine than anywhere else in France, even the Mediterranean. It was certainly true that it was as warm that October as it ever gets in Cornwall. I ripped the knees of my torn and faded jeans right through and made a pair of torn and faded shorts. It didn't matter. This really was the end of my journey. I wore them to walk up and down the beach collecting pieces of driftwood for no reason. I wore them to drink coffee in the morning, sitting cross-legged on the roof of my van, which rested in the long grass at the edge of the clearing like a horse out to pasture. In the evenings we all sat around the fire and drank red wine and ate with forks out of one huge saucepan. We washed in a disused playing field, where you could break into the shower block by climbing onto the roof and dropping down through a skylight. I took advantage of the sunshine to empty the van and clean it thoroughly from top to bottom, laying everything out on the ground in the hope that it would finally dry and stop smelling of old sneakers. I even spent half a day wiping the mold off the ceiling. Everyone said it looked much better when I finished.

In the afternoons I toured the island with Benoit in his ancient four-wheel drive Renault 4, looking for waves. I'd told him I couldn't go home until I knew how to surf and he seemed to think this was perfectly normal and offered to help me. I won't bore you with the details of my many and tiny surfing triumphs and disasters. It's enough to say that I forgot everything else again, even the fact that I would be back at Broadsands in a couple of weeks. Or, if I didn't exactly forget, I successfully pushed it to the back of my mind. I spent nearly all the money I had made in La Rochelle in the big market in Saint-Pierre-d'Oléron, the main town on the island, where I bought bread and cheese and wine to share with the others around the fire. I was still there when October turned into November. And I was still there on bonfire night, the day before my twenty-fifth birthday.

It was the day that Étienne filled up his van with all the cans of vegetable oil he had been saving up for his winter trip to Morocco. And the day the mist rolled in and obscured the sun for the first time.

"We're living in 'umidity, man," said Nadine.

It felt like the end of something, and it was. Benoit was due back at college in La Rochelle, where he was training to be a PE teacher. Jean was going to the Alps. Xavier was going to Paris to become the next Gérard Depardieu. Only Nadine was going to spend the winter at le Terrain, teaching yoga in Saint-Pierre and looking after Cash, Magic, and Silence.

There was a big party at le Terrain that night. Not because it was my birthday, although everyone agreed that it was a happy coincidence, but to mark the end of summer, in the same way that bonfire night marks the start of winter at home. Bonfire night had been Andrew's speciality. He adored fireworks, and making effigies to burn at the stake. He always chose someone we knew to model his Guy Fawkes on.

People came from all over the island to the party. Most of them were surfers that I already knew by sight. Étienne borrowed a generator from a campsite near Vert Bois. He played music on an old record player he bought in a car boot sale. Car boot sales were going to be illegal soon, he said, morosely. Or at least, you would have to declare all the money you made and pay a massive tax on it.

"*Taxer l'imagination*," said Jean.

"They want us to sell our freedom," said Xavier. "And get a death-grip."

"Mortgage," explained Étienne, seeing that I hadn't understood Xavier's translation.

Somebody came around with a massive plate of oysters. I told them I had never had oysters before and Xavier wept with laughter.

"*Bon anniversaire*," he said, handing me a lemon.

We drank copious amounts of red wine and a local spirit called Pineau that tasted like sloe gin, and then, when we were all very drunk, the generator ran out of diesel. I offered to play tapes in my van with the doors open, as long as somebody had some jump leads so I could start it in the morning if the battery went flat. Étienne said he had jump leads, and he said I should drive the van nearer to the party so we'd hear the music better. I stumbled drunkenly through the long grass and climbed into the cab. I hadn't driven it for two weeks. My lovely van. My rusty, trusty van that had once belonged to Ben's motorcross mates and then got me all the way to Nordkapp and all the way from Nordkapp to Oléron without once breaking down. Which was incredible, now I came to think of it. I leaned forward and kissed the steering wheel.

Only when I turned the key to start the engine nothing happened.

I tried again. Still nothing. Étienne went to fetch the jump leads. Still nothing.

My rusty, trusty van had finally broken down.

26

When everyone had established that what was wrong with my van was not something any of them knew how to fix, Jean called an old school friend of his called Thierry. Thierry said he could get me towed off Oléron and taken to something called the Garage Moderne. It was modern for two reasons. Firstly, if you knew what you were doing you could rent tools and lifts and work on your own vehicle for cheap, and secondly, at the weekends you would be serenaded by musicians, poets, and comedians who would come and perform for Thierry's artist friends as they sat around on the floor in amongst all the tools and bits of engine, drinking red wine and talking about philosophy and politics. Which, compared to all the garages I'd ever known, was pretty modern.

Thierry said my van needed a new starter motor. He could get a secondhand one, but it would take a while. Even with a secondhand one, the whole thing was going to cost five hundred euros. Luckily, because the garage was modern, I could work off some of it by playing my cello on Sunday nights. The rest I would have to busk for. The good news, said Thierry, was that I could stay for free in an apartment on the Quai des Chartrons that belonged to a friend of his. The only problem was that both the Quai des Chartrons and the Garage Moderne were in Bordeaux, several hundred more miles in the wrong direction. Xavier tried to cheer me up by saying that traveling theaters always kicked off a new show in Bordeaux because it was the hardest place in France to busk. He and Thierry both agreed that if I could make money on the street in Bordeaux, I could make money anywhere in the world. I was reminded of Oslo and felt sick.

The apartment on the Quai des Chartrons was right opposite the Garonne River, in a terrace of huge and dilapidated stone warehouses built in the eighteenth century by rich merchants to store their hoards of silks and spices bought or stolen from Africa. In some later century the warehouses had been carelessly split up and turned into flats. Many of the original warehouse features remained, like the unplastered stone walls, so thick that the bedroom was actually scooped out of one of them. To get into bed I had to climb a rickety wooden ladder. I brought Hanna's ribbons in from the van and hung them off the ladder. It was scarcely more luxurious than the van. There was no bathroom. There was no hot water. The cold shower was in the corner of the kitchen, separated from it by a curtain. The toilet was in another corner. The floor was tiled and the windows rattled in their frames. Instead of a fire there was an ancient leaky heater that burned petrol you had to pour into it from a jug, like a giant version of Jack's Trangia. The apartment smelled like a filling station. It was also very noisy. I had grown so used to silence that I couldn't sleep until I had unplugged the fridge and unscrewed the fizzing lightbulb in the bedroom. But I couldn't unplug the taxi drivers in the street below who spent all night leaning on their horns, or unscrew the ancient pipes that gurgled like a swimming pool.

Bordeaux is one of France's larger cities, and it was a long walk from the Quai des Chartrons to the center. Xavier wasn't joking, either. It was the worst place I had ever tried to busk. Worse than Bergen in the rain. Worse even than Oslo, because at least in Oslo there wasn't this freezing fog that came in off the sea and stayed all winter. I had never been anywhere so cold, let alone sat still for hours in it and tried to play a cello. I was worried about my cello. The cold seemed to be making the wood contract. The front and back panels were coming unstuck. There were gaps along the seams. If only I could have wrapped it up in Jack's Patagonia duck down coat. Or the red one Børge had taunted me with at Unstad.

I looked forward to Sundays, when I played in the garage, because they gave me an old gas heater all to myself. It was a strange environment for music, but I was used to that by then. I hadn't learned anything new in a while, but the big, echoing warehouse made all the old stuff sound much better. I closed my eyes and played my whole repertoire, chronologically, blending the pieces into one another. I'd start with Bach and Haydn, which would always remind me of those first awful weeks. Then I'd play "Summertime" and "Autumn Leaves" and "There Is No Greater Love," which were the long road north and the silence and the strange dusty towns like Mo i Rana, where the old people gathered on the bench to listen. Then I'd play "Vocalise" and I'd be back in Tromsø, and Jack would loom large and my heart would ache a little. I'd finish with "Bruca Maniguá," my version of it, which wasn't much like the original anymore, and I'd be back in the van with Hanna, and we'd be singing those lines from the chorus about how the answers were in the mountains. I wished I was in the mountains, too.

The whole thing took about half an hour. I wanted to learn something new, but without the van and the tapes to listen to I couldn't remember anything well enough.

Because my eyes were closed I couldn't see my poor van in the corner of the warehouse with bits of engine all over the floor. Or the audience, which was composed of the kind of designer-clad artist-hippies I've only ever seen in France, all of whom were apparently as unmoved by music as the rest of the city.

By December I was destitute. I busked and busked. I busked all day and sometimes long into the evening, too. I had chilblains all over my hands. And yet I made so little that after giving Thierry the minimum fifty euros a week I had virtually nothing left for food, let alone for the journey back to Brittany that I would have to make when the van was fixed, not to mention the ferry. But just as I was beginning to worry that I would spend the rest of my life sitting on some street corner in that big, uncompromising city, my cello in frozen pieces beside me and my van quietly rotting in the Garage Moderne, I met Romanian Georges.

27

It was the coldest day of all. So cold that nobody wanted to hang around outside for a second longer than they had to. So cold that a lady who worked in one of the posh jewelry shops on the rue Bijouterie brought me a cup of hot chocolate, evidently concerned that my fingers would actually freeze on to the strings. The hat remained resolutely empty. A tramp walked past. He spat on the pavement and told me to go and shag my mother. I packed up and wandered around the city, searching for a better pitch, but there was something wrong with all of them. Workmen were digging up the roads, doorways were full of people with clipboards collecting for charity, small choirs of children filled all the squares.

The place Allées de Tourny was unrecognizable. Rows of wooden stalls had arrived overnight as if by magic. Whole streets of them had appeared out of thin air. The stalls had roofs and heaters and big bubbling cauldrons of mulled wine and hot cider. People crowded around to buy chocolate and pretzels, and a red-faced, potbellied man in a beret was playing gypsy jazz on a dented silver saxophone while his skinny, toothless sidekick played a double bass held together with tape. People were literally throwing money into their hat, which wasn't a hat at all, but a hard saxophone case. A man wearing a blue striped apron brought them each a plastic cup of mulled wine.

The red-faced, potbellied saxophonist put down his saxophone, took a big swig of mulled wine, and stood up, the beret balanced precariously on the top of his shiny round head. He scooped out the contents of the saxophone case and tipped the coins into a leather bag, which he stuffed inside his jacket. He caught me staring at the coins.

"You are the one with the violoncello."

"Yes."

He shook his red face, took his beret off and put it back on again.

"Come," he said. "I will introduce you to my friends."

Romanian Georges led me in and out of the stalls until we came to an opening with a raised area like a tiny bandstand. He had a noisy discussion with the stallholder closest to the bandstand. The stallholder eventually laughed and handed Georges two more plastic cups of mulled wine, one of which he gave to me. Then he led me to the bandstand.

"You must not play sad music. You must play Christmas carols."

I stared at him, openmouthed. I had forgotten all about Christmas.

The place Allées de Tourny is the busiest Christmas market in France. There was a time when I would have been terrified of playing to crowds of people from a bandstand in the busiest Christmas market in France, but that time had passed. I would probably have taken all my clothes off and done it naked if it meant getting out of Bordeaux quicker.

I set up on the bandstand and launched into "Silent Night." The first phrase of "Silent Night," anyway. I made the rest up. I didn't even know if French carols were the same as English ones.

After "Silent Night" I played "Once in Royal David's City." Then I played "Away in a Manger." Finally I played 'In the Bleak Midwinter." I wasn't cold anymore. The man at the stall kept giving people cups of mulled wine to give to me. By the time I finished it was dark, I had made nearly a hundred euros, and I was so drunk I could barely find my way home.

"Silent Night" was my favorite. Over the course of the three weeks I spent on that bandstand I must have played "Silent Night" a thousand times. Nobody seemed to care. Probably because they were all drunk. I was drunk, too, every day by lunchtime. And the money just kept rolling in. By Christmas Eve I had enough piles of coins lined up on the mantelpiece in the apartment on the Quai des Chartrons to pay Thierry what I owed him and buy a ferry ticket back to England.

I drained a final cup of mulled wine with Georges and the toothless bass player. Their bus left for Bucharest in a few hours. The journey would take three days. They'd miss Christmas, but Georges didn't care. His wife had left him anyway. Divorced him because he got a passport when the Berlin Wall came down.

"It is a big world," he said. "Bigger than wife."

All they cared about was getting back in time to party all night on New Year's Eve. Which is exactly what I planned to do.

There was an old bike in the apartment. I put some change in my pocket and cycled south along the Quai des Chartrons. It was bitterly cold, which only made everything seem even more beautiful. French Christmas decorations are more tasteful than English ones. All the trees were strung with tiny white fairy lights. Fairy lights picked out the archways of the old stone bridges across the Garonne. Fairy lights lit up the road signs as the Quai des Chartrons turned into the Quai Louis XVII, which turned into the Quai du Maréchal Lyautey and the Quai de la Douane.

Finally I reached the phone box on the corner of the Quai de la Douane and the Quai Richelieu. I leaned the bike up against it and went inside. Ben answered.

"Nice of you to let us know you're alive."

"Sorry."

"Where are you?"

"Bordeaux."

"What happened to Nordkapp?"

"I went there. It was amazing. I met a girl called Hanna."

I stopped. I wanted to tell him about Hanna and Unstad and Thierry and Georges and Oléron and everything, but I didn't know where to start.

"The van broke down. I had to come here to get it fixed."

"What's wrong with it?"

"Starter motor. Fixed now."

Ben was quiet.

"How's Broadsands?"

"Crap. Just me and Jack rattling around like a gay married couple."

"What about . . ."

The words got stuck in my throat.

"Gone."

"Gone?" I gripped the receiver. "What happened?"

"She was intensely annoying. Even Jack noticed in the end, once he got bored of the sex."

I swallowed. "So he's still there?"

I tried to sound casual.

"Waste of space." Ben's broad Yorkshire vowels brought back so many memories. "On about going to Morocco or Portugal for the winter. Moaning because he hasn't got any money. Refuses to work. I've told him I'm kicking him out of the shed when you get back."

I bit my lip really hard, to stop myself crying.

"That's if you're not too busy lounging around in that yellow tin of yours with greasy Frenchmen."

I wanted to tell him I was coming home. That I really was this time. But my mouth wouldn't work.

"Fuck," said Ben. "Got to go. Customers. Come back. I miss you. I fucking need you."

"Happy Christmas," I said, and carefully replaced the receiver. There was no sweet, petite surfer anymore.

I picked up the bike and cycled blindly toward the river and the Pont de Pierre, which was built by Napoleon and is the oldest of all the old stone bridges that cross the Garonne. The river is wide at that point and the bridge is a long one, with seventeen small arches, each one hung with yet more strings of fairy lights, which made the inky river look like one of those dot paintings by Monet or someone. I was all alone. Everyone else must have been huddled up at home with their families. I had a sudden vision of them all, squashed on a thousand sofas, watching a thousand televisions, a thousand death-grips hanging over their heads.

Actually I wasn't quite alone. I was vaguely aware of another cyclist coming toward me, his big frame huddled into what looked like an old fluorescent skiing jacket. Our paths met almost exactly halfway across. He veered wide to avoid me. I

caught his eye. We both stopped at the same time a couple of
seconds later. We both turned around. It couldn't be. It was.

   "Børge!"

28

Børge lived in a tiny village called Les Torches, which perched above a larger and better-known village called Les Crevasses. Not that I had ever heard of it. I knew you took the road to Briançon from Grenoble and that both villages were in the Parc National des Écrins, right near the Italian border, nearly a thousand kilometers away.

Thierry insisted on draining my radiator and replacing the water with *liquide de refroidissement* that could cope with temperatures of −25°C and below.

"*Faites attention, huh. C'est dangereux.*"

As if to hint at things to come it had already started snowing. Thierry, who had a permanent cigarette wedged in his mouth, sighed heavily.

"Actually, I do not know why you go to the Alps in this *camion*."

"I'll have somewhere to stay."

That wasn't strictly true. Børge had simply repeated what he had said at Unstad, that if I found myself in the Alps I could park outside his house and run a heater to my van, and if he got a good picture of me wearing the Patagonia coat in the snow whilst playing my cello, then I could keep it. The coat was the reason I was going. At least, that's what I told myself. Thierry shook his head and put out his cigarette on my engine before closing the bonnet and turning the key in the ignition. The van gave a comforting roar. I climbed into the driver's seat. It had been a long time.

"She will be okay now. But if you have problems you can come back," said Thierry.

"Thank you. Thank you for everything."

He leaned in to hug me. For a moment I buried my face in his big old overcoat. I closed my eyes and breathed in the comforting smell of oil and grease. Then he let go and I was on my own again.

It had been such a strange coincidence. Børge had left Bordeaux that same night. There had been no time to meet up. No time for anything. I had cycled back to the Quai des Chartrons and sat on the floor by the petrol heater. The last thing I wanted to do was go to the bloody Alps. I studied the map in *Europe on a Shoestring*. The shed was mine again. Jack was there. There was no sweet, petite surfer. I counted my piles of money. After I had paid Thierry I would have just under five hundred euros. Enough to get to Roscoff and get a ferry from there to Plymouth. Enough to drive the hundred miles from Plymouth to Broadsands. I crossed the room and stood staring out of the window at the street below. It was Christmas Eve.

A whole week had passed before I finally gave up trying to talk myself out of it. When I said good-bye to Thierry it was late afternoon on the second to last day of the year. I decided to go across the Auvergne, so as to avoid tolls, and because it sounded romantic. It probably would have been romantic, too, in summer, when there wasn't black ice all over the road and the heater in the van hadn't decided to stop working. I had to pull over and make a hot-water bottle, wrap it in a blanket, and put it on my lap, just so my hands wouldn't freeze. The only light in the old stone villages came through the cracks at the edges of thick wooden shutters. It was far too cold to even think about sleeping. I stopped in Clermont-Ferrand to fill up with expensive diesel for sub-zero temperatures. I made a fresh hot-water bottle and spent a long time driving in circles around the industrial suburbs of Lyon. Eventually I made it to Grenoble and from there I somehow got myself on to the road to Briançon, which is when the fun really started.

The road to Briançon follows a narrow V-shaped valley, the steep sides formed out of mountains so tall and strange and uncompromising they filled me with dread. While the mountains in Scandinavia are old and worn and soft, the Alps are young, and they seemed to have all the cocky arrogance of youth. They towered over the narrow valley, folding me into their black shadows, while the snow made small mountains of the trees and spilled onto the edges of the road until I was reduced to driving in the middle of it, on the narrow strip that was scraped by huge orange snowplows that traveled up and down like beetles, lights flashing, stopping, turning, scraping again, because no matter how fast they scraped they were no match for snow like that. It fell in thick sheets, in clouds, in flakes as big as my hand, silently, eerily, relentlessly, burying everything alive. Apart from the snowplows there was no other traffic, just big flashing signs, warning of the need for snow chains, and another sign, later on, that said the Col du Galibier was *fermé*. I had never seen snow like that, let alone driven in it.

It was early morning by the time I finally reached Les Crevasses, a one-street village at the bottom of a mountain called La Mas. There were a couple of shops, a couple of cafés, a bar aptly named L'Arctique, and a ski lift. Small groups of people in brightly-colored salopettes were emerging from the cafés and heading for the lift. Next to it was a car park. I could have turned into the car park, but the cars there had been buried alive like the trees and I was terrified of getting stuck. I had to keep going until I found Børge's house. At least it wasn't actually snowing anymore. I crawled through the village, out the other side, and through a tunnel before I finally saw a sign for Les Torches. My heart sank. Les Torches appeared to be halfway up the side of the valley, at the end of a steep, single-track road with hairpin bends that had clearly not seen the benefit of a snowplow.

I paused, hovering at the junction. If I could have turned around I would have got the hell out of that valley right there and then. But the road was narrow, I was already sliding all over it, and trying to execute a thirty-six-point turn with my back wheels pointing off the edge of a precipice did not seem like such a good idea. Neither did attempting to negotiate those terrifying hairpin bends. I could see Les Torches. Being higher than Les Crevasses, further up the mountain, it was bathed in sunshine.

I wished with all my heart that I'd never met Børge. I hated him and I hated snow and I hated that stupid Patagonia coat. I cursed whatever stupid impulse had made me come to this stupid place. This death valley of orange snowplows and petrifying roads, sides so steep you couldn't see the end of them and the skeletons of trees, smothered by the relentless, suffocating snow. And now there was a car coming. I could hear it making its way toward me, then it came to the junction and sat, waiting for me to turn. So I turned. Because I had to. I turned and started inching my way up the steep road toward Les Torches, my heart bashing around in my chest like it was going to fall right out of my mouth.

My van was as wide as the road, which meant that every hairpin bend brought me inches from the edge. There were no barriers, just an increasingly sheer drop into the pit of the valley below. It was trumping everything. I was more scared than I had been getting on the ferry in Newcastle, more scared than I had been setting up outside the Nationaltheatret in Oslo, more scared than I had been in front of all those stags in the Ølhallen in Tromsø, more scared than I had been at Unstad when that huge wave had picked me up like a piece of driftwood and nailed me to the sand. One false move and I'd be dead. And it was all happening so slowly. I managed to get around the first three bends, but on the fourth I skidded. Somehow, I don't know how, I avoided sliding off the road and bouncing down the mountain to wind up in a mangled heap of twisted metal at the bottom of the valley. But the slide had caused the back wheels to come off the tracks made by other cars and dig themselves into thick snow. They spun hopelessly, and the more they spun the worse it all got. I was halfway up the steepest mountain I had ever seen, in a 3.5-ton truck, jackknifed across the road, my wheels hanging off a precipice, having not slept for twenty-four hours. And then, just when I thought it couldn't get any worse, the car I had just about managed to pass earlier came back up.

29

The car stopped. It didn't have much choice. There was a knock on my window. I lifted my forehead from where it was resting on the steering wheel and found myself looking at a man with a furrowed brow, elderly glasses, and a thick wool sweater.

"It's okay. I'm a doctor," said the man.

"I'm not hurt," I said. "Just stuck."

I climbed out of the van, trying not to look over the edge, or at how close my wheels were to it. The snow came right over the top of my boots, falling inside them and making my socks wet. The doctor had a shovel in the back of his car. He dug the snow away from the tires until the van could be straightened up and reunited with the road. He did this part, too. Then he offered to drive the van the rest of the way. I could drive his car. Which had chains.

The doctor, who was called Pierre, parked my van in a small lay-by, reversing it so the front was facing the road and the back was facing La Mas. I could see the people in brightly-colored ski pants zipping up and down it like butterflies. There was another van already in the lay-by. At least I think that's what it was. You couldn't actually see it because it was buried under so much snow. I tried not to wonder how on earth I was ever going to get down again.

"*Merci beaucoup*," I said, like a twelve-year-old.

"*De rien.*"

We both stood awkwardly in the snow.

"I am staying over there."

Pierre pointed to a small stone cottage with green shutters. It was one of many similar-looking cottages. In fact, the village was made up entirely of small stone cottages with green or brown shutters, a stone farm with some stone barns and a tiny stone church with a big stone cross next to it. In another set of circumstances I would have thought it very picturesque. The only building that wasn't made of stone was a big wooden house like the ones you see in photographs advertising expensive skiing holidays. It stood a little bit apart from the others. Pierre didn't seem to know what to do.

"You can come if you need something."

"Thank you." I wanted to grab hold of him and not let go. I also wanted to cry. Instead I said, "Do you know someone called Børge?"

"Børge?"

I reverted to English, which Pierre spoke very well. "Yes. He said he'd be able to lend me a heater."

Pierre said nothing for at least a minute. Then he said, "You haven't got a heater?"

I shook my head. It was only just starting to dawn on me, what I had done.

"Børge?" he said a second time. He took off his glasses and rubbed his eyes. "Børge lives with Rémy." He pointed to the big chalet-type house. "But I do not think he is at home. I think he is in the mountains."

"That's okay. I'll just wait for him. He'll have to come back when it gets dark, right?"

Pierre didn't reply.

I walked up to the house anyway. It was even bigger than it looked, with a long wooden veranda wrapping all the way around, a swing chair covered in snow, and a pile of snowboards that looked like they'd been there a while, just like the pile of surfboards at Unstad. I peered through a glass door at a huge fireplace and a sink full of dirty dishes. I knocked. Pierre was right. There was nobody in. It didn't matter. I didn't have to drive anymore, and I knew where he lived. Not that I could see how I could possibly park close enough to borrow a heater. But surely even Børge wouldn't let me freeze to death. I yawned. I might as well sleep while I waited.

I walked back to the van. I was too hungry to fall asleep, so I tried to make some porridge, but the milk carton was frozen solid like a brick, and you could knock yourself out with the bananas. The water in the jerry can was also frozen solid, so I filled the kettle with snow, feeling very intrepid. I tried to light the stove. Nothing happened. I shook the gas bottle. There was plenty of gas. I could hear it sloshing around. I tried again. Nothing.

I put on all my clothes and got into bed. I stared at the ceiling, which was no longer black with mold. There was something wrong with it, though. I sat up and touched it. I lit a candle and peered at it in horror. The whole of the inside of the van, which normally had a layer of condensation, now had a layer of ice. In all the corners there were tiny icicles. I lay down again, but it was like trying to fall asleep in a chest freezer. After ten minutes I was so cold I started to worry about frostbite. I sat up. I lit the rest of the box of candles and tried to warm my hands over them as if they were a fire. Outside it was snowing again, only now the flakes were like a swarm of locusts, a thick cloud of snow so dense you couldn't see through it. I couldn't see Pierre's cottage anymore, or La Mas on the other side of the valley, or Børge's house.

Who knows what would have happened if I hadn't suddenly remembered my cello.

My cello, which had essentially been stuffed in this massive chest freezer all night, without the benefit of a hot-water bottle. You didn't do that to musical instruments. You just didn't. Let alone ones that doubled up as your best friend. Ones you were depending on for your survival.

The snow was so thick I fell over three times. Twice my cello landed on top of me. Once I landed on top of my cello, falling sideways off some invisible steps. I swore that if by some miracle we both survived I would save and save for a smart new case, and I would be a normal person, and not spend my days and nights plowing through snowdrifts in a van with no heater just so I could see a man who had always made it pretty clear he didn't like me very much.

Pierre opened the door without his glasses on and wearing a clean white shirt, which made him look about twenty years younger and completely different. It was only after he pulled me inside, sat me down in a big armchair by a roaring fire and handed me a huge glass of cognac that I remembered it was New Year's Eve.

At home, the whole village went to Broadsands on New Year's Eve. Ben would move his decks into the bar. Andrew would make a vicious punch. Jack's climbing buddies would drive down from Scotland and the party would go on all night. In Les Crevasses the whole village went to Børge's. Not because of Børge, Pierre explained on the way up, but because of Rémy, his housemate, a champion snowboarder who was wearing a Hawaiian shirt and dishing out mojitos from a great silver cup that he was telling everyone he won in some competition in Canada. I was wearing one of Pierre's white shirts over the same jeans I'd been wearing all night and all day. My only pair, since I cut up my torn and faded ones in Oléron, thinking I was going home. At least I'd had a bath. My first bath in six months. I wished I hadn't washed my hair though. It stuck out like a huge afro with weird missing bits where I'd had to cut the dreadlocks out. A flock of skinny girls with fake winter tans and tiny pink dresses were hanging around Rémy. They didn't look exactly friendly. There was still no sign of Børge. I was growing more and more nervous of seeing him. He'd never have thought I'd actually come.

Pierre introduced me to Rémy, who looked me up and down in a manner that suggested he was decidedly unimpressed. He handed me a mojito anyway.

"You are the girl with the yellow *camion*."

"Yep."

"The one that was in trouble this morning," he smirked.

"Yep."

I knocked back the mojito in less than a minute and held out my cup for a refill. Rémy raised one eyebrow in a gesture he had clearly practised in front of a mirror. I didn't care. The only thing worse than being at that party drunk would be being at that party sober. I drained my second mojito.

Rémy gave me a third. After the third mojito I decided I would drive off that bloody mountain first thing, Børge or no Børge, and if I didn't kill myself on the way down I'd damn well go home, just as soon as I'd saved the money for a ferry ticket. Again. I felt a little bit better. Rémy filled my glass for the fourth time.

I decided to explore the house. I found a broom cupboard full of wetsuits, a room full of foosball, a room full of weights, and a room with a giant flat-screen television. I went upstairs. The first room I went into was obviously Rémy's bedroom. There was a whole shelf of aftershave and a rack of Hawaiian shirts. The walls were covered in blown-up pictures of himself collecting various prizes. It was equally obvious that the second room I went into was Børge's. It had a single, extra-long, unmade bed and a chest of drawers with clothes spilling out, some of which I recognized from Unstad. Hanna's book lay facedown on the floor next to a half-full mug of cognac.

I picked up the book. A paragraph had been outlined in thick pencil. It was about dying. About death being just another thought. And about being afraid of it nevertheless. I had forgotten about the way reading this book was like falling off a cliff and spinning through the air, not knowing which way was up anymore. Or maybe that was all the mojitos. I thought about Hanna. I remembered her saying that men were not the answer, and that I should stop looking back over my shoulder at the ones who had gone. I closed the book and hugged it against my chest. I wandered around the room, looking at things, touching things, trying to imagine the Børge I knew at Unstad lifting weights and watching a giant flat-screen television and sleeping in this narrow single bed. In one corner of the room was an open suitcase. It was full of clothes.

I looked closer. The red coat was in there, with a load of other brand-new Patagonia clothes. I pulled it out and put it on. It felt so warm and comforting. I zipped it up with the book inside it, pulling my arms up so the sleeves covered my hands and hunching down so it came up over my chin. I felt safe in the coat. The coat was why I had come. Maybe it was all going to be okay. The wall behind the suitcase was covered in strange wallpaper. I leaned in for a closer look and saw that it wasn't wallpaper at all but photographs, hundreds of them, and all of the same person—a pretty blonde girl with a crooked mouth. Børge was in some of them, standing next to her, and he was actually smiling, his arm slung around her shoulders. And then I saw something familiar. I hunched down further into the coat. In almost every photograph the girl was standing in thick snow with skis on. But in this one she was on a beach, holding my surfboard, the one Børge had given me at Unstad. Wearing my wetsuit.

A shadow landed on the wall in front of me.

"What the hell are you doing?"

Børge's voice was dangerously quiet. I made myself turn around. He was standing in the doorway, his massive frame blocking the light.

"Who told you to come in here?"

"I'm–"

"Get out."

There was an expression of disgust on his face. As if he hated me.

"Get OUT!"

30

I woke up in Pierre's armchair, still wearing the red coat. My head was trying to push itself through my skull. I made it to the bathroom just in time. When I had finished throwing up I crossed the living room and went to stare out of the window at the blizzard. By now my van had also disappeared under the snow.

I went back to the armchair and put my head in my hands. I moaned softly to myself. To think that I could be waking up safe and warm at the hostel, with Jack close enough to touch and Ben making a fry-up in the kitchen, the smell of bacon wafting into the bunkhouse, an old reggae record on the decks and Andrew rolling joints on the bar. Except Andrew wouldn't be there, of course.

I closed my eyes. It was a long time since I'd been this hungover. It was worse even than Tromsø and the day after the night I spent with Henrik. If only I'd been drunk enough to pass out and not remember anything. Instead I couldn't stop thinking about Børge's face when he found me in his bedroom and the way he'd pinned himself to the side of the door frame so I wouldn't accidentally touch him as I squeezed past, still wearing the coat, with Hanna's book zipped inside it. Everybody had been clustered around Rémy, counting down the seconds to midnight. I ran past them and out into the snow and kept on running until I fell over and Pierre picked me up and brought me to his cottage.

Oh God! What had I been I thinking? But what kind of psycho papers their bedroom walls with pictures of their ex-girlfriend? Maybe he was mentally ill and everybody knew it except me. That would explain a lot.

Pierre eventually got up. Without saying anything he gave me some acetaminophen and a bowl of milky coffee with cognac in it. He kept going over to the window and staring out of it for ages at a time and not saying anything, then turning around and looking at me and rubbing his chin. I picked up Hanna's book and read a sentence. It made no sense whatsoever. I put it down. Maybe I was the one who was mentally ill. Pierre was still pacing.

"Are you okay?" I asked.

"Si."

"I can go back to the van."

"*Non, non. Trop froid.*"

Eventually Pierre put on his skis and said he was going to Les Crevasses. When he had gone I went and stood by the window myself. I looked across the valley at La Mas. Pierre said it was one of the deadliest mountains in the French Alps, as well as the highest. All the runs were off-piste and dotted with obstacles like trees and rocks and the huge crevasses that gave the village its name. That day the peak was hidden behind a blanket of swirling snow.

I put on my wet boots, Pierre's jumper, and Pierre's big duffel coat that was hanging by the door and came down below my knees. I carried the red coat in a plastic bag. I couldn't wear it anymore. I passed the old stone barn. Cows were coughing and fidgeting inside. I passed the church. The snow was so deep every step was an effort, but I kept going until I reached Børge's house. I crept on to the veranda and left the plastic bag hanging from the door handle. The fire was out and there were no lights on. The big room was full of the devastation of the previous night. Empty glasses covered every surface. A rug had been rolled back, presumably for dancing. There were people asleep on both of the sofas.

In spite of the swirling snow, I wanted to be outside. I walked down a tiny lane that branched off the main one just after the church. It was hard going, pushing through the blizzard, sliding around on the icy lane. Finally I reached another stone hamlet, tinier even than Les Torches. The lane turned into a track that turned into a path that followed the bank of a frozen river. The blizzard had eased, and I could see now, but I was still wading up to my thighs in snow. After what felt like a very long time I came upon two ruined stone cottages. Beyond them there was a rickety wooden bridge. Beyond that there was nothing but mountains, folding endlessly into one another as far as the eye could see.

Mountains, help me find the paths of freedom.

I stood on the bridge for a long time, staring at the water moving under the ice.

Pierre came with me to the van. He said the regulator on top of the gas bottle had air in it, which had frozen. If I put a hat over it to warm it up the cooker would work fine. He ran his fingers over the thickening sheet of ice that covered the inside of the fiberglass ceiling. Night was falling.

"But you cannot sleep in here."

I leaned on the side of the van, utterly exhausted. The mountains were so silent. Somewhere a dog howled. It was impossible to tell if it was close or far away. Or maybe it was a wolf. Pierre said there were wolves in the Parc National des Écrins. I went back to the cottage with Pierre and slept on the floor in his duck down sleeping bag. He tried to persuade me to let him sleep on the floor so that I could have his bed, but I wouldn't let him. He had already been far too kind.

I spent the following day in Pierre's cottage. I didn't go outside. Pierre went skiing and I read Hanna's book, which was comforting, even though I still couldn't make head or tail of most of it. In the evening some friends of his, called Sergio and Kevine, came to the cottage. They were musicians. Pierre made me unpack my cello. Sergio played a drum, eyes closed, joint balanced between his lips, long black dreadlocks swinging gently in time to the music. Kevine had a guitar, and he played gypsy jazz like Django Reinhardt. I didn't know what to do. I sat holding my cello and not playing it until they had finished. Pierre took the joint out of Sergio's mouth and handed it to me.

"But you're a doctor!"

"*C'est la médicine,*" said Pierre.

Eventually I played "Bruca Maniguá." They knew it and pretty soon they had both joined in. They didn't know the words though, or the history. I told them what Hanna had told me, about it being a song about oppression, sung by the descendants of black slaves in Cuba.

"I think all music is about freedom," said Sergio. "I think music is freedom."

They taught me a new tune that night. It was called "Kasbah Tango" and it was by an Australian group Sergio had heard of called Trio Alegra. It had a kind of melody that's so perfect it keeps you awake at night, running itself round and round in your head. We played it over and over and over. Sometimes I played the bass and sometimes I played the melody. We all kept our eyes closed while we were playing. Pierre made us endless cups of coffee with cognac and smiled like a child.

"Why did you come to Les Torches?" Kevine wanted to know.

"I met a guy called Børge at a place called Unstad. We were surfing. He told me that if I came here he'd take a photo of me wearing this coat and I'd be able to keep it. Then I saw him again, halfway across the Pont de Pierre in Bordeaux. It was weird. That's why I came. And now I'm here I can't go. My van is buried in snow. I'm trapped." I glanced at Pierre.

"Børge?" said Sergio.

"It was a strange coincidence, don't you think?" I said, defensively.

"*Une vraie coïncidence,*" said Kevine, who was small and dark and had two Italian parents.

"*Faites attention,*" said Sergio. Be careful.

It was deep into the early hours when Sergio and Kevine left. Pierre and I watched them crunch off through new drifts of thick snow that had fallen while we were playing. There was a big moon and the sky was so clear and cold it literally took my breath away.

"You are smiling," said Pierre. "It is better."

"I love that tune."

"Your violoncello is your friend, I think. Perhaps your lover."

"We've been through a lot."

31

It was a week before I saw Børge again. Pierre persuaded me to go with him to L'Arctique one night, to watch the screening of a film called *La Trace de l'Ange*, about a man called Marco Siffredi. He promised me Børge wouldn't be there.

"He is always in the mountains. Nobody has seen him since the party."

L'Arctique was full of people with red faces standing around in snow clothes and drinking beer from high wooden tables. Marco Siffredi was a teenager with white hair from Mont Blanc, who had been the first person ever to descend from the peak of Everest on a snowboard. The film was projected onto the back wall of the bar, where Marco launched himself off the roof of the world laughing, as if life were a game. Incredibly, he survived. Then he did it again. They never found his body. When the lights came on everyone was crying.

I looked for Pierre, who was no longer sitting in the chair beside me. He was at the bar, talking to a tall man with a rucksack on his back. I looked away quickly, but it was too late.

Børge crossed the room and sat down next to me in Pierre's empty chair. His clothes looked like he'd been wearing them for a few days. His slate-blue eyes were bloodshot. He seemed desperately tired.

"You're still here."

"I'm stuck. My van's stuck."

"Pierre says you are sleeping in his cottage."

"That's why I'm still alive," I said.

"Do you like the mountains?"

"Yes."

Silence.

"Actually I love them."

"Have you tried skiing?"

"Nope."

"I said I'd take you."

"It doesn't matter."

"Thanks for leaving the coat. Do you still want it?"

I looked up at him. His curly dark hair had snow in it, as if it had gone gray overnight.

"That's why I'm here," I mumbled.

Børge came to Pierre's cottage the following day. Pierre had already gone out. If we were to get a good photograph, Børge told me, we would have to spend the night in one of the ruined cottages further up the mountain. The ones I had accidentally walked to on New Year's Day. The cottages belonged to the national park. Since Børge was employed by the national park, as a guide, he had keys. We had to wake up there, he said, so that we could get a shot at first light. The cottages were basic. We'd ski in, towing food, sleeping bags, and the cello behind us on a toboggan.

"Aren't you forgetting something?"

"I don't think so," said Børge.

"I don't know how to ski."

"Okay, we'll go tomorrow. Today I will teach you how to ski."

It was Unstad all over again. We went to the baby mountain, where the under tens go, and Børge watched me fall over. Again and again and again. One leg going one way and the other one going the other way until I landed hard in the middle, on my bum.

"I fucking hate snow."

"Just be patient. It'll come. It's much easier than frigging surfing."

"I can't fucking do that, either."

The following afternoon, by which time I was pretty much just one big bruise, I was deemed ready. Luckily, Børge was towing the toboggan. Also, because most of it was uphill, we were actually mainly walking. It was hard work.

"Careful not to fall in," Børge shouted, as I veered much too close to the river.

An early dusk had descended by the time he unlocked the door to the farthest cottage. Inside was a wood-burning stove with a pile of logs on the stone floor next to it, dust, spiders, two chairs, and an ancient table with a rotting blue top that reminded me of old French films, and a pile of books that Børge said were his. There was another floor, but you couldn't get to it, because the stairs had rotted through.

"Do you often spend the night here?"

"Yep. Rémy likes to party. I don't."

"Where do you sleep?"

"On the floor."

Børge went outside and chopped an armful of logs. He lit the stove and pulled a saucepan and a bag of pasta out of his rucksack. I peeled off the waterproof trousers I had borrowed from Pierre and lay on the floor in front of the stove, my feet pressed against the metal. Børge stood in the open doorway, looking at the darkening mountains.

"You said you were going back to England."

"I was going back to England."

"What changed?"

"I saw you on the Pont de Pierre."

"You thought it frigging meant something?"

I sat up. I was angry.

"No. I wanted the coat."

"You could have just bought one in a shop. It would have been cheaper."

He crossed the room and sat down at the table. He looked like a giant, squashed onto one of the tiny chairs in his big coat. I got up off the floor and came and sat opposite him.

"It was your idea. Why did you tell me to come, if you didn't want me to?"

"I don't know."

"You told me to come twice. You said you would lend me a heater."

"I thought I was over it, okay?"

"Over what?"

"You saw," he said roughly. "When you came in my room. You were looking at her."

"The girl in the photographs? The one you're stalking?"

Børge clenched his fists

"I'm sorry," I said, "I didn't mean to say that out loud."

"She's dead."

32

"I'm so sorry," I said at last.

It all made sense now. All of it.

"When? I mean what happened?"

I wanted to touch him, hold his hand or something, but I didn't dare.

"Two years ago. The first of January."

"New Year's Day?"

"I didn't know you were going to frigging turn up then."

"Shit."

"I'm sorry I shouted at you."

"I'm sorry I was nosing around in your room. I was drunk."

"I should be over it by now," said Børge. "I thought I was over it, until you turned up at Unstad."

I felt like someone had nailed me to my chair.

"I hated to see you wearing her wetsuit."

"I know. I could tell. Why did you give it to me?"

"I decided to get rid of her stuff. To get closure." He laughed, but not because anything was funny. "Only there you were, hanging around, wearing it every day right in front of me. She was like you, too. Mental. Afraid of nothing. You even look a bit like her."

I stared at him. He shook his head.

"The way you came knocking on the bus and asking for a board like that. You didn't even know us. The way you got back in the sea after the size of that set that took you out the first day. The way you tried to drive that frigging van of yours up to Les Torches with no chains."

He smiled. He actually smiled. "She was just like that."

I was silent. Did I tell him I was scared of everything? That when I knocked on the door of the bus my heart was thumping so much I could hardly breathe? Did I tell him that when my van got stuck on the way up to Les Torches I was seriously considering hurling myself off the edge of the mountain and putting myself out of my misery once and for all?

"What happened?" I muttered, instead.

"We were skiing on La Mas. Hungover. She was caught in an avalanche. I went to get help. There was a blizzard. I couldn't get back to her. She died alone. We found her body the next day."

I thought about Andrew. I tried to imagine if he'd been my lover instead of my friend. Børge got up and went to the door. He opened it and leaned on the frame.

"I should never have left her," his voice cracked slightly. "That's the thing I can't get over. She should have died in my arms."

"You would have died, too."

"Maybe I should have."

"It's not your fault," I said.

He came and sat down again. It was cold. I got up to close the door. The moon was rising, yellow like an awful sun. I stared at the terrible beauty of the cold empty night. I could just make out the edges of the mountains under cloudy layers of stars. There were no lights anywhere. I wanted to go to him, hug him, anything. I wanted to make it better. But I knew I couldn't. This was life. This was the way it was.

"I thought I was ready," he said.

"Ready for what?"

My mouth was dry. I noticed the way his mouth turned down at the corners. I shivered.

"Are you cold?" he asked.

"A bit."

He got up and went to his rucksack and pulled out the red coat.

"You might as well wear it."

It was like being safe in bed under a thick duvet.

"Shall we eat?" I said, finally, after a long silence.

The pasta had congealed into a single solid lump.

"Dinner's kind of fucked," I said, poking it.

I brought it over to the table. We looked at it.

"I'm not hungry anyway."

"Neither am I."

"I knew someone who died," I said. "The whole busking thing was his idea. That's why I did it. I felt like I owed it him to do something with my life. Because I still had one and he didn't."

"It was the opposite for me. I wanted to be dead."

"Do you think that's what she would want?"

"No, I guess not. Maybe. I don't know." He shook his head.

"You said you were running away."

"That, too. Both."

Børge was looking at me like I was some kind of lifeline. I had to keep talking.

"Life is complicated. Not like books, with heroes and villains and one simple reason for doing things. It's more like a big, scary wave, like that one that got me at Unstad. You have to try to ride it, because otherwise you'll die, and sometimes it's easy, but other times there's all these long, dark sections, and sometimes you don't make it, and sometimes you think you're not going to make it but you do, and sometimes it just closes out and it's not your fault."

Børge was sort of half-smiling.

"Keep going."

"And every time you think you've nailed it and you know how to do it something else comes along, something you never expected, to throw it all up in the air again. There's no finishing line."

Finally I understood.

"So you ended up at Unstad because of this guy who died."

"No. I ended up at Unstad because of Hanna."

"Who's Hanna?"

"The girl who gave me that book. She wrapped me up in light."

"She what?"

"She wrapped me up in light." I grinned. I knew how it sounded. I knew nobody would ever believe me. "Honestly. It was the best feeling ever."

"Better than sex?"

My eye caught his by accident and I found I couldn't tear it away. I could hear myself gabbling on, but it sounded like somebody else.

"She taught me not to look backward and wish things were different and she said I had to live my life like it was the best book I ever read."

Børge's slate-blue eyes looked different when he smiled. Much less cold.

"You and your books. Like that crazy one you lent me."

"Do you get it?"

"No. But I like it anyway."

"Me too. Sometimes when I close my eyes and think about it really hard it kind of makes sense. There's all this stuff out there, all swirling around together and instead of enjoying it for what it is, we make up words for things that don't exist and then call them good or bad."

If only I could shut up. Børge evidently felt the same. He leaned forward and put a finger to his lips.

"Sssh."

"Sorry."

We gazed at each other across the table.

"Why did you come here?" he said at last.

"I keep telling you. I wanted the coat."

"Is that the only reason?"

There was a long silence. I found myself thinking about the time I caught Jack's eye across a candle in his shed. I knew then that something important was going to happen. And something important had happened. If it hadn't been for Jack, I would never have gone to Norway. I would never have met Hanna. I would never have come to these mountains. I hadn't had what I wanted from Jack, the happy ending I'd read about and watched in films. But maybe all this was better. Maybe what I got was better than what I wanted.

The truth was like a door that suddenly opened in my head.

And in that moment of clarity, before the door closed again, I knew that whatever I was doing up there in those mountains with Børge had some purpose, too, and I didn't even have to worry about what this purpose was, I just had to play my part, and I also knew that whatever came out of this thing with Børge, it wouldn't be anything like what I expected. Børge's eyes were blue, like Jack's. It was hard to remember Jack's eyes, actually, now that I was looking at Børge's.

That was the truth. Only I couldn't possibly put it into words, so instead of answering I leaned over the table and kissed him. We kissed for ages. We kissed until I couldn't stand up and Børge had to scoop me up and carry me over to the fireplace, where he laid me on the floor and we carried on kissing.

33

I must have fallen asleep, because when I woke the fire had almost gone out. I sat up.

I slowly remembered everything that had happened the previous night. The things Børge had told me. The way his girlfriend died. The way he had scooped me up and carried me to the fire like a baby. I realized he wasn't there. The door was slightly open. I kicked myself out of my sleeping bag and reached for the red coat, which was hanging off one of the chairs by the table. Børge's bag was still there, leaning up against my cello. I pulled on my boots. The night was outrageously cold. The air felt solid. The snow was hard under my feet. Nothing moved. There was a big, bright moon that hung like a disco ball, throwing stars everywhere. Layers of stars. I saw him standing on the bridge, leaning over the rickety wooden railings, staring at the icy river.

I began to walk toward the bridge, but before I got there I stopped. He hadn't seen me.

It was not my business to be there. I turned and began to walk back to the cottage, hurrying, not wanting to be seen. That's probably why I slipped. I slipped on some ice. I heard something go crack. It was so cold I almost didn't feel any pain, but I must have made a noise, because Børge was running toward me, slapping my face, telling me it didn't look good.

He insisted we go back to Les Torches immediately. He made a sling out of a spare pair of boxer shorts and wrapped me in the red coat, doing up the zip around my arms as if he was dressing a dummy. He picked up the cello and marched me outside.

"You might go into shock. You need to be warm and dry."

"It's fine," I tried to say, and sat down in the snow. Waves of nausea kept bubbling up. Tears fell hopelessly out of my eyes. Bugger, bugger, bugger.

"Get up," Børge snapped.

Gone was the person I had been kissing. Back was the angry young man I had met at Unstad.

"I'm tired. I wanna resht for a bit."

I was slurring my words.

"Frigging get up. Unless you want to die out here."

Part Four:

The Ribbons Are for Fearlessness

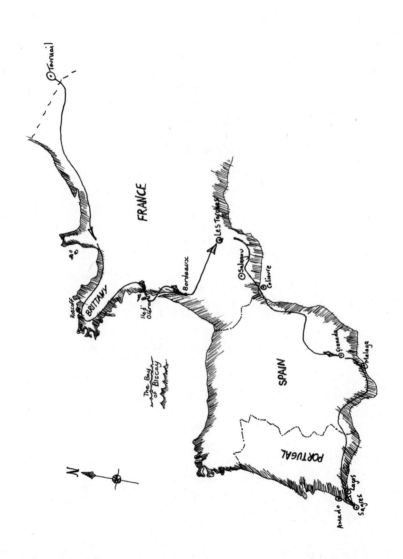

FRANCE

BRITTANY

Roscoff

Tournai

Bordeaux

Iles d'Oléron

The Bay
of Biscay

Les Toghes

Salagou

Collioure

SPAIN

Granada

Malaga

PORTUGAL

Amado

Lagos

Sagres

N

34

Pierre confirmed what we both already knew. My right arm, my bowing arm, was broken. Badly broken. I had to get to a hospital. In France you pay for hospital treatment and then claim the money back. If you have a valid E111. Which, it turned out, I didn't. I'd said in the post office in England that I didn't know exactly how long I'd be away, but that it would be about three months. They told me to make up a date and then Tipp-Ex it out later if I needed to. When I managed to explain what Tipp-Ex was, Pierre looked horrified. This was France, he said, you didn't put Tipp-Ex on official documents, even if you knew what Tipp-Ex was. He rubbed his chin. Hospital treatment would be expensive. There was one other option, he said, but we'd have to leave immediately.

Pierre gave me some morphine.

I woke up on the Rue Saint-Pierre in Marseille, opposite the Hôpital de la Timone.

"How did we get here?"

"We drove."

"How did you get the van out of the snow?"

"We dig it. Børge help me. We work all night. Then we use his chains." Pierre showed me the chains, which were lying in the footwell.

"Where is he? Is he okay?"

Pierre looked sad. "Not really, but I think you have helped."

It was too much to get my head around, even if it hadn't been full of morphine. I gave up and slid back into unconsciousness.

The nurses were surprised to see Pierre. He wasn't due back from holiday for another week. They clearly liked him, though. He gave them a big bar of chocolate and they helped him smuggle me in and out of X-ray. After the X-ray he marched me down a dozen corridors, stopping to hold the negatives up against a window, tut and shake his head. He marched me past a huge queue of the injured and desperately bored, his white coat billowing authoritatively, and through a pair of double doors that slammed shut behind us. The bone specialist, who'd been up all night like us, was drinking a cup of tea. It wasn't a simple break. I was lucky not to need an operation.

Back in the van I looked helplessly at Pierre.

"Two months. I can't even drive." Let alone busk, I thought. All I wanted to do was sleep.

"It's okay," Pierre said. "I know somewhere you can go. My uncle has a big house on a lake called Salagou. He will like you. You have *le feu*."

"What's that?" I slurred.

"Fire."

My head slid slowly down the inside of the window. I closed my eyes. After all that, I had left without the coat.

Salagou was a man-made lake a few hundred kilometers north-west of Marseille. Pierre's uncle lived in an old, stone house. Unkempt vines trailed over rotting wooden frames and the big paved terrace that looked out over the lake could have done with sweeping. The house was called La Soleiade, which Pierre told me meant "place of sunshine," and the sun was warm already, in spite of it being a few days shy of February. It was hard to believe I was in the same continent as Les Torches, let alone the same country. Gone were the cold, stark mountains and in their place was a weird desert of scorched red earth and huge canyons. I was struck with a kind of homesickness, a gray sense of loss that made me want to sit down on the ground and put my head between my knees and weep. Instead, I let Pierre park my van under one of the rotting wooden frames and hustle me inside.

Pierre's uncle was a short man with a ruddy face and Pierre's kind eyes. His name was Francis Philippe. Francis Philippe had worked for many years selling antiques. Everything he had not managed to sell he had stored at La Soleiade, presumably awaiting the time when it would be reduced to ashes by some apocalyptic volcano several billion years hence. Every room was overflowing with a mixture of junk, books, inappropriate furniture (beds in the kitchen, wardrobes in the lounge) and defunct electrical equipment.

My homesickness increased as the two of them showed me around. Not that I knew what I was longing for exactly. I thought about Broadsands, and Ben, and Jack, like picking a scab and trying to make it hurt. But oddly enough it didn't hurt, or at least not like it had. I thought about Børge. I hoped he wasn't blaming himself for my accident. I hoped I'd see him again one day. But that wasn't it, either. I knew deep down that Børge wasn't ready yet, that I'd only have got tangled up in his pain if I'd stuck around.

We came to a bedroom. It had a large double bed, a couple of antique cots, an incongruous desk that looked like it might have come from IKEA, if they'd had IKEA in the 1930s, a washbasin, and a porcelain chamber pot. Pierre and Francis Philippe left me and went downstairs. I lay on the bed and stared up at the ceiling. There were spiders in all the corners, hanging off ancient, dusty webs. Pierre had been so kind. I was so lucky. I was safe and warm and dry. I turned on my side to face the wall. I remembered all those times lying on the bed in the van and counting out my stacks of coins. I thought about the tunnel in Bergen and the bench of elderly people in Mo i Rana and the strange German shopping centers that let you play for twenty minutes at a time and all those endless drives across alien countries, and washing in rivers and service stations, and how desperately I had wanted it to be over and to be safe and how desperately I missed it now that it was.

It was thinking about my cello that did it. My cello had been with me from the very beginning, had been my friend, my companion, my survival, seen me through the darkest times. And now, just when I needed it most, when it was the only thing I could think of that would make me feel better, I couldn't play it. My fingers itched with frustration. I sat up suddenly. In fact, where was my cello?

Pierre and Francis Philippe were sitting in the kitchen, drinking tumblers of red wine. I burst in, gabbling incoherently, tears streaking my face. It was a few minutes before Pierre was able to understand what I was going on about. He led me outside and opened the van. The cello was stashed safely in the cupboard, right where it should have been. I leaned against Pierre, unable to stand up. He put his arm around me.

"It's okay, *ma chérie*. Børge bring it back."

As if he could read my mind, Pierre pulled it out and opened the case. I started crying again. Because wrapped around the cello, tied carefully around the neck as if to keep it warm, was the Patagonia coat.

35

In the end I slept in the van under the rotting wooden frame. Francis Philippe made a fuss, and had me borrow the porcelain chamber pot, but I think he liked it really, this display of *feu*. He liked the fact that I was a gypsy. I just wanted to go home, and I finally knew that the van *was* home, more than anywhere else had ever been. In the morning Pierre arrived.

"I come to say good-bye."

"You're *going*?"

"I have to collect my car," he said. "And then I have to go to work."

"I ruined your holiday. I'm so sorry. And thank you. You've been so kind. I don't know what I would have done without you."

He blushed slightly. "It's nothing."

"Will you see Børge?"

"Yes. I expect."

"Will you thank him, for the coat?"

"Of course."

"And tell him I'm not coming back."

Pierre took my hand and held it gently. "I tell him already."

"What did he say?"

"He say maybe he see you one day."

What Francis Philippe liked to do most was wander the shores of the lake searching for edible plants. I'd watch him go and watch him come back from an old wooden rocking chair on the big, paved terrace. I had very little energy that first week at La Soleiade. All I could do was sit and stare at the water, watching birds carefully dragging bits of grass and moss out onto the surface to make small island nests for themselves. Even though it was warm during the day, I wore the red coat constantly, snuggling down into it. I slept a lot, something Francis Philippe encouraged, and ate strange food that he said would make me strong, containing things he found on the shores of the lake. Wild herbs and a stringy vegetable that he said was wild spinach. Wild leeks and wild mushrooms. Francis Philippe made his own bread, which was invariably so stale he had to chip away at it with a meat cleaver. The nearest shops were many miles away, and his car was so old he preferred not to drive it. Instead, Pierre brought supplies from Marseille when he came to visit on his days off.

Considering that our communication was limited by the little we knew of each other's language, Francis Philippe and I got along very well. After my need to sleep had worn off, I tried to earn my keep by doing things around the house. I found an old CD player and stack of dusty CDs. Among them was an old John Coltrane album and I fell in love with a track called "In a Sentimental Mood." It was a long, slow piece of jazz, not smooth at all but full of air, like a meditation. It seemed to be neither sad nor happy, neither major nor minor. It wasn't going anywhere, either. It just meandered along like a river, and every time I listened to it everything felt like it was going to be okay. I listened to it over and over while I swept the terrace and cleaned out the fridge. I would have hoovered the cobwebs, but there was no hoover, so I had to make do with an ancient antique feather duster, holding it awkwardly in my left hand, trying not to catch spiders in my hair.

The first week passed slowly, achingly slowly. At the end of it Pierre came with fresh bread and smelly cheese and an old bicycle he had borrowed from one of the nurses. Pierre strapped my cast to my chest with an old bandage, found a rusting old bike of Francis Philippe's, turned it upside down, mended what seemed like a thousand punctures, oiled the brakes, loosened up the chain, and took me on a long ride around the lake. To cheer me up, he said.

It was a beautiful day. We followed an old path that often thinned to nothing and disappeared, forcing us to dismount and carry the heavy old bikes until we could ride again. It was hard at first with only one arm, especially to stop, but the exercise felt good, and by the end of the day Pierre had me laughing.

"You just have to be patient, *ma chérie*."

After that I went out on the bike most days, exploring every inch of the lake, finding the remains of drowned villages and feeling inordinately happy to see the first buds pop out on trees I didn't recognize. In the evenings I took to sitting on the terrace and drinking wine with Francis Philippe. He told me about his life and read me odd things from the ancient books that sat in piles all over the house. Once he showed me photographs of his wife, collected in an old album with yellow lace trimming. Francis Philippe told me she had died of cancer nearly ten years ago. It still upset him to talk about it. Pierre was in some of the photos, a younger, fresh-faced Pierre, on holiday from medical school, with a pretty brunette hanging off his arm. Pierre's wife, Francis Philippe said. His childhood sweetheart. I was amazed.

"Pierre has a wife?"

"He had a wife. She left him for another doctor. One of his friends."

"Oh God, poor Pierre!"

"He was very sad, but he is happier now."

"Pierre deserves to be happy," I said.

Francis Philippe looked at me with this old-fashioned expression he'd use from time to time, but he didn't say anything.

Sometimes Pierre would take me out for the day in his ancient Polo Coupé, which went by the name of Paulette. We went to Montpellier and sat on the Place de la Comédie and drank hot chocolate. We drove high up into the Cévennes, where it was cold, and ate steak and potatoes by a roaring fire. The first of March came and went. One unseasonably hot day we took Paulette all the way to the Camargue to see the flocks of pink flamingos and drink cocktails on the beach. It was here that Pierre told me his plan.

"I have a holiday in two weeks."

"My cast comes off in two weeks."

"I know," said Pierre. "That is why I think you should have a holiday, also."

I shook my head. "As soon as the cast comes off I've got to start busking. I've got almost no money left, and I've got to get all the way back to England. It's going to take forever."

It was a daunting prospect, especially when Pierre said, gently, "You know your arm will need some time, some physiotherapy. You will not be able to busk immediately."

It honestly hadn't occurred to me.

"How long do you think it will take?"

"I do not know. Until we remove the cast we cannot know if it has healed."

"You mean, it might *not* have healed?"

"I am sure it will be okay, but you must give it time."

"I *can't* give it time."

"That is what I am telling you. I have an idea. I have always wanted to be a hippie."

"I don't believe you."

"It is true. I would like to be hippie in your *camion*. I would like to take my holiday with you in your *camion*. I will pay for the diesel and you can do exercises to make your arm strong enough to busk. I will help. In return you will allow me the opportunity to be hippie. I have always wanted to do this."

I was speechless. Partly because of how incredibly kind and thoughtful Pierre was, and partly because of the dawning realization of how tough things were going to be. Pierre was right. At the very least, my arm would be wasted and weak. It would be ages before it was capable of the long hours of busking I used to do. And I would be horribly out of practice. And that was if it had even healed properly. You heard all sorts of stories about bones not healing, or healing funny and having to be rebroken and set all over again. In all the weeks at La Soleiade, I'd tried not to think about my cello, but now the thought of it hit me in the ribs where it hurt. I longed to play it. I longed for those old tunes and the sense of peace they brought me. It was like a hunger.

"Where shall we go?"

"I have always wanted to see the Alhambra," said Pierre.

"Where's that?"

"Granada."

"Spain?"

"Southern Spain."

"*Southern* Spain?"

"I thought you were busking from Norway to Portugal."

"No, no, that's what Andrew was going to do. But he's dead. I want to go home."

Home seemed so far away. Broadsands was part of another lifetime. I was veering so far from my old life I was afraid I would never find it again. It was months since I had spoken to Ben.

"We can go to the beach. We can walk in the Sierra Nevada," said Pierre.

That night I asked Francis Philippe if I could use his telephone to call England. I offered him the tiny bit of money I still had left over from Bordeaux, but he brushed it away, offended. The telephone was an old-fashioned one with a round dial you had to turn with your finger for each number. Ben sounded unhappy.

"I should have called."

"Yes."

"I'm sorry."

"You missed Christmas."

"I know. I broke my arm."

"Fuck," said Ben. "How?"

"I fell over on some ice."

"In Bordeaux?"

"In the Alps."

"The *Alps*? You're in the Alps?"

"Not anymore. I'm by a lake in the south of France."

"I give up. You know you're totally illegal now."

"What do you mean?"

"No tax, no inspection, therefore no insurance. If something happens you're completely screwed."

This stuff hadn't even crossed my mind.

"I opened your tax letter and did the SORN thing for you, so at least you won't get a massive fine."

"Shit. Thanks."

"I suggest you throw away your MOT certificate. If you get stopped just show the insurance and the registration document. You'll probably be okay."

I bit my lip.

"We were worried about you. We almost called the police."

"Seriously?"

"We talked about it."

"Who talked about it?"

"Me and Jack."

They were worried about me?

"Is he still there?"

"Nope."

I caught my breath. "Where is he?"

"In Portugal."

"Why?"

"Why do you think? Surfing his brains out, as usual. When are you coming back?"

"I've got to go to Spain. It's a long story."

"You're not coming back."

"I am coming back. Just not quite yet."

After I said good-bye to Ben, I went outside and sat in the dark on the terrace in the old wooden rocking chair. I sat and stared at the darkness for ages, until Francis Philippe came and turned on the outside light. Huge moths hurled themselves at it. Somewhere far away a dog barked. He put a moth-eaten blanket on my lap.

"What is the matter?"

"Nothing," I said.

"You have bad news?"

"No, I don't think so. I don't know."

What was the matter? Was it that Jack had left again? He'd come back. He was only in Portugal. In fact, he was closer to me in Portugal than he was at Broadsands. Anyway, what did I care about Jack any more? Now that there was Børge, and Pierre. Pierre? I was overwhelmed by feelings I couldn't put into words. That was what music was for. That was what my cello was for. I needed to play my cello. My good hand was clenching into a fist. I had never gone this long without playing my cello. If only I could just sit there in the dark and play "Bruca Maniguá." If I could just play that, I would feel okay again.

"What are you thinking about?"

Francis Philippe was kind. I think he was worried.

"My cello," I muttered. "I miss it, I suppose."

Francis Philippe shuffled off. He came back with an old guitar, which he placed in my lap, on top of the blanket.

"I can't play the guitar."

"Pierre said it would help you to try to use your fingers."

I picked it up. With my left hand I tried to find the melody from "Bruca Maniguá," but the guitar was tuned differently from the cello and it didn't work. I tried to pick the strings with the fingers of my right hand, but they were all seized up. It was like trying to open a gate whose hinges had rusted solid. God only knew what would happen when I actually did try to play my cello. I didn't want to think about it. I put the guitar on the floor. I stared at the darkness.

"There's no point."

"You must have courage, *ma chérie*."

I folded my arms. I heard Hanna's voice in my head and I wanted to stick my fingers in my ears. Instead I found myself almost shouting.

"I'm bloody sick of people telling me to have courage. I'm sick of it. Fucking courage and fearlessness. Look where it got me. I can't do anything. I'm completely fucking useless. Fear is there for a reason. To stop you trailing off through the fucking mountains and breaking your arm and fucking up your cello . . ."

Francis Philippe shook his head. "Do you know what courage is?"

"Doing all those things you don't want to do because you're too bloody scared. Probably because they're so fucking dangerous."

"*Non non non.*" Francis Philippe straightened up and walked over to the edge of the terrace. He looked down at the lake for a while, then he turned to face me.

"Courage is not about what you do. Courage is about keeping your heart."

I shook my head.

"*Si*. Courage is from *coeur*. *Coeur* means heart."

I had never seen Francis Philippe look so serious. He marched out of the room again and came back with a yellowing old book. It was a huge Latin dictionary.

"Courage," he read aloud, "means to be who you are with your whole heart. To tell the story of who you are with your whole heart."

There was a pause, while the words sunk in.

"And how are we supposed to do that?"

"With music, for example. Playing the cello, for example. Or being a good doctor, like Pierre. Or a good wife, like my wife, for example."

"I can't play my cello."

Francis Philippe picked up the guitar and put it back in my lap.

"Then you will have to sing."

36

I sat there for hours that night, picking away at the guitar, trying not to turn around when Francis Philippe shuffled in to check on me. It was for his sake, really, that I tried. I tried to write a song about Jack, a love song about loss and pain, but it was crap, and what I actually ended up writing was a song about Hanna. And it was good to be reminded of her, to remind myself of the things she had taught me, remind myself that I was free.

Even when I had most of the words I couldn't think of a melody, so I went to bed with it going round and round in my head like a puzzle. In the morning I knew what I had to do. It took most of my last two weeks at La Soleiade to learn to play the chords to "Bruca Maniguá" on the guitar, and then fit the words of my song about Hanna to them. It seemed appropriate, but it wasn't easy. Mainly because I couldn't play the guitar and I had to learn each and every chord from scratch, and also because my right arm was in a cast and the fingers that poked out of the end of it were so wasted that even trying to pluck open strings was a massive effort of will. I'd hum the song and try to match the chords and hope that Francis Philippe wasn't listening, which I knew he was, and smiling to himself, because I seemed so much happier and the whole thing had been his idea. And then the two weeks were up and it was all over.

Pierre cut the cast off himself with a penknife. My arm was yellow and covered in thick black hair. I was nearly sick when I saw it. Pierre seemed to think it had healed well, even though I could barely lift it up. I tried not to show how shocked I was. At least the fingers sort of worked, thanks to the guitar. Pierre opened a bottle of champagne to celebrate. After the champagne we drank two bottles of red wine from Francis Philippe's cellar. It was the end of March. The vines had sprung back to life. The birds had hatched their chicks on their little islands in the lake.

"Do you want to try to play your cello?" said Pierre. "I will get it."

"No!"

I was terrified I wouldn't be able to.

We left the following day. Francis Philippe folded me into a bear hug and gave me the ancient guitar as a leaving present. I tried once again to give him what remained of the money I had made in Bordeaux, but once again he wouldn't hear of it. I was all choked up and couldn't say good-bye properly.

"There is always a place for you here," he said. "You have *le feu*."

Pierre drove and I sat safely strapped in on the passenger seat with nothing to do but stare out of the window at the landscape drenched in sunshine and the meadows full of flowers and the foothills of the Pyrenees in springtime.

I would have stopped and hung around in some meadow, but Pierre refused. Spain was a big country and Andalucía was away down in the south of it and he had a plan written down in the "notes" section of his guidebook. He insisted we kept going. In the early evening, after the Pyrenees finally folded into the Mediterranean, we stopped for the night at a small seaside town near the Spanish border called Collioure, a place of narrow cobbled streets, old wobbly houses and sandy beaches. It could have been St. Ives except for the fact that the sea wasn't cold, and instead of surfers the beaches were full of tables spread with tablecloths and wineglasses and great heaving piles of shellfish waiting to be boiled alive.

We left the beach where we had swum, drunk wine, and eaten freshly boiled shellfish, and walked up a flight of steps to the van, which was parked so that we could see the sea from the back step. I had missed the sea. The sky was inky blue, and a perfect slice of moon dithered on the horizon. Pierre picked up Francis Philippe's guitar and began to gently strum some soft music that made me think of warm southern nights and starlit streets. He could play quite well. I closed my eyes. After a while the music stopped, and I realized that Pierre had begun to very gently stroke my face.

I kept my eyes closed. It felt good. It didn't feel important, or dramatic. It just felt good. Which was so confusing I pulled away.

"It's too complicated," I said.

"What is complicated about sex?"

"I don't want to spoil everything."

"We are friends. Why can we not also make love?"

Pierre was still stroking my face. It still felt good.

"Unless you do not want to."

I did want to.

"But then what?"

"I think love is like a good cheese," Pierre said. "You enjoy it when it is ripe and then you forget about it."

My mind fought with itself. I had slept with Henrik. But I knew I never had to see Henrik again. And I had been very drunk. I had been in love with Jack. Maybe I still was. And Børge, well, there was that meeting on the Pont de Pierre, and the way I felt when I looked at his eyes. I didn't have that same feeling about Pierre, the feeling that there was some *purpose* to it. He was just nice. The nicest man I had ever met. Did that mean I should sleep with him or I shouldn't? Maybe there *was* no should and shouldn't. Maybe it was all just up to me.

"Sometimes I feel like life is this big game, only just when I think I'm getting the hang of it the rules change and I have to start all over again."

"I had a wife."

"I know. Francis Philippe told me."

"She had a lot of rules. Now I do not have rules. Because rules are always wrong. Trust me, I'm a doctor."

Nothing happened that night, but we fell asleep together in my bed, side by side, and in the morning I woke with my head on Pierre's shoulder, as if it were a pillow.

We left Collioure and followed the coast to Barcelona, stopping at roadside bars for espressos and freshly squeezed orange juice, drinking them standing up while flies pecked at our heads and swarthy truckers wiped the sweat from their foreheads with paper napkins. Just before we hit the city we turned inland and began to head toward Albacete and the

Sierra de Segura, a range of mountains a little lower and further north than the Sierra Nevada. Night fell. The road emptied. Pierre decided to take advantage of the empty road and drive all night. I drifted in and out of sleep. In the early hours of the morning I was woken by the sound of sirens and Pierre shaking me and asking me for my documents.

Pierre was calm, but then, he would be. I was having a mild heart attack, remembering what Ben had told me when I called him from La Soleiade. I hastily flicked through the papers, trying to surreptitiously remove the ones that were out of date. Fortunately Pierre, who could speak Spanish as well as everything else, distracted the policemen by chatting to them through the open window. I handed over the registration document, the insurance document, and my passport. Pierre seemed blissfully unaware that, even if my insurance certificate had been valid, he wasn't on it. The policemen glanced at the papers. They breathalyzed Pierre and asked to see his passport. It was in the back, so he gave them his identity card instead.

"You're a doctor?"

"Yes."

It was nearly as good as having a cello. They handed back all the documents without reading them and sent us on our way.

There was a national run on drink driving that Easter in Spain. Pierre got breathalyzed four times that night, and each time the police asked to see my documents. It was so ironic. Apart from the English policeman who kicked my tires at the Tyneside tunnel, nobody had once asked to see my papers in all the months I had been away. Until now, when half of them were out of date.

I could see why the police were doing it. I counted thirty wooden crosses by the side of the road, each one piled up with bunches of flowers. Each one another Andrew, with dozens of shell-shocked friends and a grieving family. I remembered what Hanna had said about *all* the moments being precious. She was right. Life was so short, and so fragile.

After the fourth time he was breathalyzed, Pierre gave up. He bought a sack of oranges from a stall on the side of a steep road and pulled into an empty, dirty lay-by.

"Welcome home," he said, handing me an orange.

I felt like a newly released prisoner, sitting there on the back step and staring at a long view of mountains, only this time they were dry and dusty, with orange trees that smelled of jasmine and skinny goats with bells on scratching themselves on piles of old stones that must have been houses once, and olive groves and a hazy sky stretching out over sweeping valleys and the sun spilling over the mountaintops and warming our faces. I closed my eyes. There was the sweet smell of manure.

"The best thing about being a hippie," I said, opening my eyes again, "is the view."

37

Perhaps it was because Pierre was expected back at the hospital in six days' time and was already booked on to a flight from Málaga, while I was responsible for getting this rattling old yellow van back to England, a journey some thousand kilometers in the opposite direction. Or perhaps it was the fresh goat's cheese wrapped in paper and spread on the warm flatbread we bought from the same men who sold oranges by the side of the road. Whatever the reason, I decided to sleep with Pierre, and this time I didn't regret it.

We traveled slowly over the dusty mountains. We had sex by lazy rivers. We sat in shady bars in tiny squares and ate chorizo and olives. We drank jugs of sangria in the middle of the day and had sex on the roof of the van. We wandered hand in hand through tiny whitewashed villages, and in the long, warm evenings Pierre played soft, warm music on Francis Philippe's ancient guitar and, because he made me, I began to play my cello again.

It was hard. At first I couldn't get my fingers to grip the bow properly. I kept dropping it. I wanted to cry with frustration. Pierre showed me some exercises I could do to build up the muscles in my hand, and I did them obsessively, whenever we were driving, drumming my fingers on the dashboard and squeezing the gear stick over and over. I tried to play all the things I used to busk, but they sounded terrible, and reaching the end was an effort of will that left me tense and shaking. Pierre massaged my shoulders.

"Let's play together."

He picked up the guitar and strummed a few easy chords. I put down the bow and used my wasted fingers to pluck the strings instead. I found the bass notes of the chords, closed my eyes, wrapped my arms around the cello, and tried to get lost in it.

"That's better," said Pierre.

"Only because you were playing, too."

After that I gave up trying to play the old stuff. It was too depressing. Instead I began trying to work out the John Coltrane tune called "In a Sentimental Mood" that I had listened to so much at La Soleiade. I couldn't listen to it anymore, so I had to shut my eyes and try to remember it, hearing the phrases in my head, one by one, and linking them together like a jigsaw (or making bits up when I couldn't remember), and because each phrase was new I didn't mind playing it over and over again, which was easier for my hand than trying to play the whole of "Vocalise," say, and not being able to get to the end. And in any case, this particular tune didn't seem to be about getting to the end. It was more like a dream. You could dip in and out of it, and it was just sweet and lazy and sounded beautiful. As the days passed and I kept on trying, I began to notice an improvement. My hand got stronger. I could play for longer. I could play faster. I stopped dropping the bow. But it was a long, slow process, and I was dreading the day Pierre got on that flight from Málaga and I had to busk again.

At the bottom of the Sierra Nevada we found the Costa del Sol. Everyone knows the Costa del Sol is a ruined place. Ruined by the electric-gated concrete mansions and the high-rise hotels, the golf courses and the orange tans and the beer-vomit on the beaches. I had expected all that. What I had not expected were the wild places that still exist in between the sprawling suburbs. It wasn't quite the snaking rivers and empty mountains of Scandinavia, but we did find empty beaches with no paths to them, where we could swim in clear water and have sex on hot, white sand. And on the steep climb back up to where the van was parked in an empty roadside lay-by, we picked armfuls of wild thyme. We played music on the clifftop and fell asleep listening to the sound of the sea. Admittedly we were invariably woken in the middle of the night by gangs of noisy youths on mopeds, who used the lay-by as meeting place for all manner of illegal activity in which the police invariably thought we were involved. But Pierre was a doctor and I had a cello, two things that never failed to reassure them that we were respectable citizens and not drug smugglers, after all.

One morning towards the end of our week together Pierre made me play the cello for him. He made me play for twenty minutes, as if I was busking. He used his watch to time me and lay on the ground listening, his hat pulled down over his face. I got through it. I played "Autumn Leaves" and "Bruca Maniguá" and Sergio's "Kasbah Tango," and I finished with the John Coltrane.

"Good," he said, at the end of it. "You are ready."

"It still sounds awful. And my hand hurts."

He made me stretch my fingers out and then make a fist and then do this quickly, twenty times.

"It is okay. You will live."

"You really think I'm ready for the street."

"I do not think the street is ready for you, *ma chérie*."

38

We reached Granada on 8 April, forty-eight hours before Pierre was due to fly home from Málaga. I drove that last leg. I hadn't wanted to drive. It was easier to be a passenger. To let Pierre decide where we went, and how fast, and where we stopped. But Pierre insisted. I had to climb back into the driver's seat and grip the steering wheel and take charge of my own destiny again.

I drove slowly and it felt surprisingly good to be driving my big old van again. Like meeting up with an old friend after a long break. While I drove, Pierre read out loud from his French guidebook. He wanted me to know about the Alhambra, which was an ancient Moorish palace "overgrown with wildflowers and grass in spring."

"I like the sound of that," I said, stroking Pierre's leg. "Sounds like the Pyrenees."

"Watch the road!"

Pierre continued reading, "The Alhambra was built as a paradise on earth, but the reconquista forced the Moor kings out of Spain and the Christians took it."

The Alhambra was not a paradise on earth. The car park cost fourteen euros and the queue stretched a mile. After three hours even Pierre had had enough. He left the guidebook in the van and we walked arm in arm through the gardens to the town, listening to the nightingales.

"It is your fault," said Pierre.

"How is it my fault?"

"You make me lose my plan."

"You said you wanted to be a hippie. Hippies don't have plans. They go with the flow."

We spent the afternoon wandering Granada's narrow streets, which heaved with tourists. It was Good Friday and Granada was the scene of a huge religious procession. To escape it, we walked away from the center and found ourselves in a wide tree-lined square at the top of a steep hill. The square was filled with old stone benches. The whole city was laid out beneath us, like a three-dimensional map. Pierre pointed at clouds gathering over the mountains.

"Thunder," he said.

I sat down on one of the old stone benches.

"What's wrong?" asked Pierre.

"Nothing."

"Something."

"You know my friend who died."

"Andrew."

"He died just before Easter. He's been dead for exactly a year."

Pierre pulled my head onto his shoulder. "Not really, Easter moves."

"You know what I mean."

I got up and went to lean over the stone wall that ran around the edge of the square. Pierre had been right. I could hear thunder rolling around in the mountains to the north. A flash of lightning ripped the sky apart, followed by another low rumble. Pierre came and leaned over the railings beside me. I could smell the sweet smell of rain falling on hot tarmac.

"There were so many things he was going to do before he died."

"Like busking from Norway to Portugal," said Pierre, who liked the word *busking*. There is no such word in French.

"Yes, like that."

"So why do you go back to England?"

"What do you mean?"

"Why don't you busk to Portugal?"

"You can't really busk from Norway to Portugal. It's ridiculous. It was bad enough just getting to the midnight sun. Especially now. God knows how long it's going to take me to get back to Brittany. I can only play my cello for about ten minutes at a time and it sounds totally hideous."

I really didn't want to think about busking. Pierre grabbed my hands and pulled me up off the bench.

"But *ma chérie*, you are nearly there. It is only one thousand kilometers to Sagres."

"*Only* a thousand kilometers!"

"Do you know how far you have come? How many kilometers?"

I shook my head. "No."

There was another bolt of lightning, this time followed by a massive crash, followed by the sound of clouds breaking and dumping several tons of water on our heads. Pierre grabbed my hand.

"Come on!"

When we had changed into dry clothes Pierre opened a bottle of wine and filled two mugs. I lay beside him on the bed, resting my head on his shoulder. He was so solid and comforting. He was staring at a map he had bought just after we left Salagou. A road map of Europe. He had been horrified that I didn't already have one.

"How didn't you get lost?"

"You can't get lost if you don't know where you're going."

Pierre just shook his head and asked me if I had any paper. I pulled some pages out of an old notebook and lay back down on the bed, eyes closed. I didn't even ask why he wanted it. The day after tomorrow Pierre would be gone. I would be on my own again.

Pierre wouldn't let up. He made me tell him all the places I had been, every town I had busked. Eventually I sat up, curious to see what he was doing. He was sketching, making these little hand-drawn maps, one for each section of the journey. And on each map he was marking the places I had busked and the distances between them, which he worked out using the edge of a piece of paper, just like we used to do at school in geography lessons. He finally reached Granada.

"Fourteen thousand kilometers."

I drained my mug of wine and stared at him. "Fourteen thousand kilometers?"

"Yes. Look."

He stuck the maps on to the tongue and groove with toothpaste, side by side, and traced my route with his finger.

"Norway, Finland, Sweden, Denmark, Germany, Holland, Belgium, France, Spain. Nine countries. Nine countries and fourteen thousand kilometers. Approximately."

I was genuinely shocked.

"I didn't really do the whole thing busking though. You paid for me to get here, and to Marseille from the Alps. And Francis Philippe fed me for two months."

Pierre rubbed his chin. "I think it is the same. I do all this because you play with Sergio and Kevine with your eyes closed. It is because you play your cello that I fall in love with you."

"You *what*?"

"It does not matter. You have come fourteen thousand kilometers and you have one thousand left. You must not give up. You must go to Portugal and find the Cabo San Vicente and say good-bye to your friend."

He raised his mug. Eventually I raised mine, too.

39

I wept when I said good-bye to Pierre at Málaga's tiny airport.

"*Bonne chance, ma chérie.*"

He stroked my face one last time. I wanted to grab hold of his shirt and never let go, but he walked briskly through the barrier and I couldn't touch him. All I could do was watch him get smaller and smaller until he disappeared.

I wept again when I got back to the van. Pierre had left me with a cupboard full of food, a tank full of diesel, his road map of Europe, and all the little maps he had drawn with the places I had been marked on them. He had even drawn little pictures based on the stories I had told him. There were strange-looking musk oxen in Trondheim, and a thin girl with huge eyes sitting cross-legged at Knivskjellodden. There were surfers at Unstad, Danish forests, German truckers, and his little cottage in Les Torches. There was Collioure and the Alhambra. And there was a new map that he must have done in the night, while I slept. It was of what lay ahead of me, blank, apart from the distance, a thousand kilometers, and a picture of a lighthouse at the end of it. I poured some cold water into a mug, leaned out of the back door, and splashed my face. I had to pull myself together. I climbed into the driver's seat, put "Bruca Maniguá" in the tape player, and set out to finish my journey.

Of all the ten countries I traveled through, Spain was the only one I didn't busk in. I had been planning to stop in Seville, but the traffic jams into the city were so bad the van overheated and I had to sit for hours on the hard shoulder waiting for it to cool down. I tried to distract myself by playing Francis Philippe's guitar and singing my song about Hanna:

You said you wrapped me up in light that day,
You said you'd show me how to find my way . . .

It was evening by the time I reached the border. There were half a dozen border police wearing a mixture of Portuguese and Spanish uniforms. The police were waving most of the cars through, not even stopping them to check passports. My rusty old van was another matter. Three of them flagged me down. I handed over my passport, my registration document, and my invalid insurance certificate. The policemen frowned at them, shook their heads, kicked a few tires, and told me to open up the back.

It was the Tyneside tunnel all over again. Except it wasn't. That time the van resembled a disused sauna, with mold all over the ceiling. This time it looked like a home. The red tin teapot and two mugs were stacked in the washing-up bowl that was also a sink. Sunlight fell on Francis Philippe's ancient guitar, which was lying on the bed. The ceiling was free from mold, washed even cleaner by the ice. Hanna's book lay on the piece of sawn-off plywood. My embarrassing pairs of underwear were drying on a piece of string that Pierre had nailed to the tongue and groove. They looked like prayer flags. One of the policemen asked me to open up the cupboard. He even made me open the old, beaten up case. Then he laughed, gave me back my papers, winked, slapped me on the shoulder, and let me go.

I traveled slowly along the Algarve. At first it reminded me of the Costa del Sol, carved up by golf courses and sprawling concrete complexes, purpose-built for tourists. But the old towns were still old, and the beaches were mainly empty, and even in Faro fishermen went to sea in colorful wooden boats.

I spent the night on the top of a cliff and the following day I busked in Portimão. In the evening I called Pierre from a pay phone. It was strange hearing his voice. I told him that busking was all right after all. The Portuguese were not rich like the Norwegians had been, but they were not mean like the French. They liked buskers. I told Pierre that I had set up outside a café and one of the waiters had brought me an orange juice on a tray, as if they had hired me to be there.

I called Pierre every day that first week. I told him about the old men who got drunk and sang Fado at night on the street. I told him that Fado was the saddest music I had ever heard, and how it made me feel better about playing "Vocalise," only what I mainly played was "In a Sentimental Mood." I didn't tell him this was because it reminded me of him. Neither did I tell him that now that I was in Portugal, every time I saw a tall blond man my head would spin and my knees would go weak and I'd have to sit down. Not that Jack would be in some big, dusty town in the Algarve.

I had given up trying to make sense of it all. Life was far too confusing.

Instead I studied Karen's *Stormrider* surf guide. I was heading to Sagres. This was where Andrew's lighthouse was. There were beaches there where you could surf. And there were more beaches all the way up the west coast. I was nervous. I had almost forgotten all about surfing.

After a week in Lagos, the last of the big Algarve towns, busking every day for crowds of Easter tourists, I tipped the contents of the biscuit tin out onto the bed and counted my money. I had about two hundred euros. It was time for the final leg of my 9,300-mile journey.

40

I left that afternoon, driving west, on and on, past Vila do Bispo and then out along the flat, straight road to Sagres. It was a bit like the road to Knivskjellodden. Not quite as empty, of course, but wild and with the same feeling of driving right out to the edge of the world. For it was another edge. The southwestern tip of Europe, with nothing on the other side of it but thousands of miles of empty ocean. Sagres felt like a frontier town, too. The trees were bent double from the wind and half the roads were dirt tracks. There were surf shops on the main street and signs to half a dozen beaches. There were plenty of signs to Cabo San Vicente, right out at the end of the empty, straight road, with high cliffs on one side dropping down to the ocean, and scrub on the other.

There were vans like mine in the car park. Rusty vans with wetsuits hanging off broken wing mirrors, surfboards stacked on roofs, scruffy-looking dogs. I could see the lighthouse clinging to the land for all it was worth.

I climbed out of the van and stood on the tarmac. The sun was sinking and the wind was cold. I shivered in my torn and faded shorts. I opened the back doors and pulled on my red duck down coat. On an impulse I went back into the front and picked Hanna's ribbons off the rearview mirror. I stuffed them in my pocket. I didn't bother with shoes. I walked barefoot toward the white-washed lighthouse and the end of the story.

Outro

And then it was all over. Except it wasn't, because endings are as hard to pin down as beginnings are, and every ending is also a beginning.

If this was a romantic novel I would have bumped into Jack on the long, sandy beach called Amado where I fetched up after Cabo San Vicente. The car park was a dusty field full of vans and tents and surfers, and the sun was so strong it burned my eyes. Every time I got out of the sea and climbed back up the crumbling cliff I couldn't help but imagine he'd be standing there by my van in a pair of jeans and a flat cap he'd bought in some charity shop, with an old rucksack by his feet.

"How did you know this was my van?"

"Ben told me to look for a giant yellow rust bucket."

"How did you know I'd be here?"

"Ben again."

"Ben didn't even know I was coming to Portugal."

"He said you'd be in Sagres."

I'd put the board down and try to unzip the wetsuit. But the zip would be stuck.

"Come here."

Jack would tug it down, his fingers brushing my skin.

"Since when did you learn to surf?"

"Since Norway."

"Did you really go to Nordkapp and see the midnight sun?"

"Nope. I went to Knivskjellodden. It's even further."

"Why didn't you let me take you surfing?"

"You never asked."

Jack would offer to buy me a beer and we'd walk to the village and sit on red plastic chairs and drink Sagres and eat peanuts.

"Where are you staying?"

"Dunno. I've got a tent."

"Are you flying back from Faro?"

He'd pull his cap down over his eyes. "I was thinking maybe we could go back together in your van. Surf our way up the coast."

I'd let myself imagine it. Lying in his arms with my head on his shoulder, his hand resting on my knee while he drove, like Pierre's had. But then the dream would fall apart, because we'd be laughing, like Pierre and I used to laugh, and I couldn't remember ever laughing like that with Jack.

I stayed at Amado for a month. Every weekend I went back to Lagos and busked for two days, making enough to live on for a week. Sometimes people would come with me. Surfers who made and sold jewelry, or played guitars, or made things out of driftwood. It turned out that there were plenty of other people on my path, after all.

I could have stayed at Amado forever, and I almost did, but one of the surfers I was friendly with had to go back to England and offered to pay the diesel if I would drive him in the van.

I went to Lagos one last time and busked until I had enough for a ferry ticket to England, and then I drove with him across Portugal and Spain and over the border into France, and all the way back to Brittany, and the whole thing took two days.

I didn't sleep on the overnight ferry from Roscoff. Instead I stood out on deck and watched the sunrise from the back of the boat. I was alone. The surfer I had given a lift to lived in London, so he was catching a ferry from Calais. This time I didn't need Stan and his bottles of warm white wine to keep me from crying. I stared down at the water slipping away beneath me, like time, and I thought about my cello, and how the first thing I was going to do when I got back was find someone to stick the seams back together. And I thought about my van, and how I still didn't have a spare tire, or an MOT certificate, and how I didn't even care.

I snuggled down into my red Patagonia coat, which was better than Jack's, and put my hands in the pockets. Hanna's ribbons were still there. I shivered slightly. For all I knew Jack was still in Portugal. I hadn't called Ben. I didn't know what to say.

Instead of going to Broadsands I went straight to the beach.

The fog was so thick I couldn't even see the sea, I could only hear it. It was just like Knivskjellodden. I pulled on my wetsuit and paddled out anyway. Surfing is a hard thing to learn, because you never get the same wave twice. I was still very much a beginner. But at least I could catch waves before they had broken, and get to my feet most of the time, and ride them in a straight line toward the beach. Which is what I was doing when I saw Jack.

I fell off and went under, and when I came back up there he was, paddling toward me. I barely had time to spit the water out of my mouth and clamber back on my board before he was right there in front of me, one of his big hands reaching for my board and pulling it toward him until we were sitting side by side, bobbing around in the fog together. And his hands weren't that big, after all, and although my heart was thumping like a train, I realized that the Jack of my imagination didn't exist, and the Jack right there in front of me was just a man, and a scared one, and I'd have been willing to bet that his heart was thumping like a train, just like mine.

"Where did you learn to surf?"

"Norway."

"Only you could grow up in Cornwall and learn to surf in Norway."

Jack had walked to the beach, so I gave him a lift up to Broadsands in my van. First he wanted to look in the back. I felt proud. Even in the heavy fog, my van had the feel of summer, as if some of the bright sunshine of Amado had found its way permanently into the pores of the wood. Hanna's book lay facedown on the plywood offcut that served as my kitchen. Jack picked it up and read the first page.

"Where did you get this?"

"Someone gave it to me. You can borrow it if you like."

"Thanks."

He bit his lip just like he used to. We looked at each other. And I saw that Jack's eyes were not slate blue after all, but light blue and sort of watery, and he wasn't half as tall as Børge, and his eyes didn't have laughter lines that joined up with his mouth like Pierre's had.

"So?"

"So."

"How was yours?"

"You went first."

"Oh, you know. Full of Spanish. Fucking cold."

I almost laughed out loud. I'd forgotten how Jack used to hate everything. A couple of girls walked past the van, carrying the foam surfboards you learn on. I could feel them looking at him.

"How long have you been gone anyway?"

"A year. I left a month after Andrew died."

I still couldn't believe Andrew wasn't going to be there, rolling joints in the bar, with a pint of Guinness next to him, reading *The Surfer's Path* and taking the piss out of all the articles.

"Let's go."

Ben would understand.

I drove, with Jack slumped on the passenger seat. I went over the speed bumps slowly.

When I had left there had been banks of flowers by the side of the road. There were no flowers anymore.

"What was her name?" I said, breaking the silence.

"Who?"

"The girl you lived with in the shed. The one you brought back from Patagonia."

There was an uncomfortable silence.

"Topsy," he said at last.

"*Top*sy?"

"She's American."

"When did you meet her?"

"Right away. I should have told you. I guess I was in love. I wasn't thinking much about anything else."

I stared in front of me at the road. Love.

I wish I could feel you naked beside me.

I pressed play on the tape player. It was halfway through "Bruca Maniguá."

"I took your tapes," I said. "I listened to them all the time."

"What tapes?"

"The ones in the box you left behind. You said I could have them."

"They weren't mine."

"Whose were they?"

"I dunno. I must've got them in some car boot or something."

Ben came running out wearing his chef's cap and hauled open my door and pulled me out and gave me a massive hug, so massive my feet left the ground. He smelled of the old days, of chip fat and marijuana.

"Someone said they saw a big yellow van at the beach."

I mumbled something about Rattler and being tired and then we were all sat in the bar and Jack was skinning up and it was like none of it ever happened.

"Can you work tomorrow?" said Ben. "I've got a load of people arriving."

I took a few moments to answer. I looked around at the crumbling paint and the empty bottles lined up on the bar and the fog staring in through the windows.

"I don't mind working tomorrow. But I don't want my job back."

They both stared at me.

"What are you going to do?"

"I don't know. Busk in Truro, I suppose. Go away again."

"You'll have to pay rent."

"Why?"

"That's the deal. If you want to live here and not work."

"I don't want to live here."

"Where will you live?"

"In my van."

Ben and Jack looked at each other.

"I need some time out," I said, and had to put my hand over my mouth to stop myself giggling uncontrollably. I knew if I started laughing I would never stop.

"What happened to you?" said Ben, crossly.

I tried to tell them about Hanna, but it was just like the old days. They took the piss.

"She sounds like a Bond girl."

"I'd give her one."

"Maybe if you gave her one you'd get ribbons, too."

So I gave up trying to talk to them and instead I went to my van and got the ancient guitar that Francis Philippe had given me at Salagou, and I went back into the bar and I sat down and I started to play the chords from "Bruca Maniguá," the song that will always remind me of Hanna and that night we drove through the wilderness together. And then I started to sing the words I had finally finished writing on the long journey home. And it certainly shut them up. They stared at me like I was a freak of nature, and I could hardly blame them. I used to die of shame if one of them accidentally heard me playing my cello through the thick walls of the bunkhouse, and now here I was singing in public.

You said you wrapped me up in light that day,
You said you'd show me how to find my way,
You said these moments are all precious,
And the ribbons are for fearlessness . . .

It wasn't easy. I had to stop and take a big swig of Rattler, which is when I noticed they weren't taking the piss any more.

"What is that?" asked Ben. "It's really familiar."

"It's an old Cuban song. Ibrahim Ferrer did a cover. That's probably why you know it. I used it loads busking. That girl I was trying to tell you about got me into it. In fact, this song is about her."

"How can an old Cuban song be about some girl you met in Norway?"

"They're my words."

Jack and Ben looked at each other.

"Start again from the beginning," said Jack.

V.1

YOU SAID YOU WRAPPED ME UP IN LIGHT THAT DAY
YOU SAID YOU'D SHOW ME HOW TO FIND MY WAY
YOU SAID THESE MOMENTS ARE ALL PRECIOUS
AND THE RIBBONS ARE FOR FEARLESSNESS
YOU GAVE ME A BOOK ABOUT SIMPLICITY
AND YOU TOLD ME I WAS FREE.

CHORUS.
SO I TRAVELLED FOR YEARS WITH MY SONGS
AND I FOUND ALL THE RULES TO BE WRONG
AND ALTHOUGH I WAS FAR FROM HOME
I KNEW I WAS NEVER ALONE.

V.2
YOU SAID YOU WRAPPED ME UP IN LIGHT THAT DAY
YOU SAID YOU'D SHOW ME HOW TO FIND MY WAY
YOU SAID THESE MOMENTS ARE ALL PRECIOUS
AND THE RIBBONS ARE FOR FEARLESSNESS
THEN YOU WRAPPED ME UP IN LIGHT
AND YOU LOST ME IN THE NIGHT.

Acknowledgments

Although I did this on my own, I could never have done this on my own.

I have been blown away again and again by the warmth, generosity and kindness of humans, just a few of whom I have listed here.

I owe a massive debt of gratitude and love to my blood relations—Terry, Daisy, Colin, Naomi, Rosie, Tristan, Tamsyn and Barnabas—for being the most eccentric and inspiring bunch of people anyone could hope to belong to. I would also like to thank my non-blood relations—Kirstan Gorvin and Ben Vavrecka—for being top brothers.

I'd like to extend huge thanks to David and Jane Cornwell for their initial support and continued encouragement and advice. I'd also like to thank Rebecca Winfield, for believing in me and for offering such excellent editorial notes, and everyone at Summersdale for being so positive and taking such a lot of care, particularly Jennifer Barclay and Sophie Martin. I am grateful to Mark Watts for so readily granting me permission to quote from his father's book.

I'm indebted to everyone who helped with the van, especially Henry Dowell, whose week-long carpentry workshop and general off-grid friendship will never be forgotten—not to mention the rusting weapon, which would have got me out of all sorts of scrapes if everyone hadn't been so damn friendly.

I'd like to thank all the countless people who offered me support, both emotional and physical, during my year-long journey, but most especially Jan Inge Hellesmark and Philippe Schott, whose extraordinary kindness completely changed the way I feel about the world. And I will never forget JB, whose words and ribbons I still treasure and strive to live up to.

Back home I'd like to thank my extended Penwith family for the hot showers, houses, parties, vegetables, doors, dances, stoves, surfboards, bread, cheese, chocolate, shelving, paid work, books, and laughter. You are too numerous to list here, for which I am eternally grateful, so I will just single out those who were most directly involved in keeping me sane(ish) during the many stages of this project. Emma Bohadana for the clothes and the counseling, Dave Spenceley for the nuggets of music and wisdom, Becky Martin for listening and sharing the shed thing, and Will West for living with me and feeding me and making sure I didn't completely forget how to have fun.

I want to thank everyone who has helped with the EP, especially the incredibly talented Richard Blackborow, whose patience and generosity knows no bounds, and Alan Shepherd, whose encouragement has been invaluable.

And finally, I want to thank Ashley Moffatt for the inspiration.

Photo by Mike Newman

About the Author

Catrina Davies was born in Snowdonia and grew up in the far west of Cornwall. When she isn't surfing her way around the world, she divides her time between writing and music.

The Ribbons EP, a collection of songs that helps to tell this story, is available through the author's website: www.catrinadavies.co.uk/ribbonsep (or scan the QR code below).

She currently lives in a tin shack near Land's End, where she is working on her second book and recording her second album.